D1335121

Lake District

Berlitz Publishing Company, Inc.
Princeton   Mexico City   Dublin   Eschborn   Singapore

Original Text: Lindsay Bennett
Editor: Christopher Billy
Photography: Pete Bennett
Cover Photo: Pete Bennett
Photo Editor: Naomi Zinn
Layout: Media Content Marketing, Inc.
Cartography: Ortelius Design

Although the publisher tries to insure the accuracy of all the infor-
mation in this book, changes are inevitable and errors may result.
The publisher cannot be responsible for any resulting loss, incon-
venience, or injury. If you find an error in this guide, please let the
editors know by writing to Berlitz Publishing Company, 400
Alexander Park, Princeton, NJ 08540-6306.

ISBN 2-8315-7173-1
First Printing April 1999

Printed in Italy
019/904 NEW

CONTENTS

- A  in the text denotes a highly recommended sight

Lake District

THE REGION AND ITS PEOPLE

Tucked away in the northwest corner of England, 240 km (150 miles) from London, the Lake District nestles just below the Scottish border and backs up on the Irish Sea. At just 2,300 sq km (3,710 sq miles), the area is small enough that it can be covered by car, north to south, in just a few hours. This little corner of England is such a beautiful and valued region, however, that policy makers and conservationists have worked tirelessly over the last hundred years to protect it. The label the "Lake District" is actually a little misleading. Although there are in fact many bodies of water, much of the charm of the region lies in the landscapes produced by the high peaks, majestic valleys, swathes of forest, and rugged fells (highland plateaus or pastures) that surround the lakes. It is an English landscape that has enchanted many, from hardworking farmers and sheepherders to vacationing naturalists to resident poets. The area's natural beauty continues to inspire writers and artists. Visitors come not only to view the mountains and the lakes but also to hear the words of poets who lived here and to learn about their lives.

After considerable study and touring in the Lake District, German scientist Rainer Bramer declared that the region had the best views in the world. He asserted that the area was blessed with the highest concentration of exactly those natural features that, when combined, create the most pleasing and relaxing vistas possible—landscapes composed of "lakes representing the source of life in water, trees offering the promise of shelter, smooth areas providing easy walking and a curved shoreline or path in the distance to stimulate curiosity." Native Lakelanders and visitors alike know exactly what Bramer was talking about.

For such a small tract of land, the geology of the Lake District is actually very complex. The oldest rocks are 500 million-year-old slates found around the northern peak of Skiddaw, where the mountains have smooth and rounded profiles. Only a little farther south, around Langdale Pikes, for example, the terrain is formed of volcanic rock; much younger and more dramatic in appearance, these mountains have rough crags and sharper peaks. At the southern extremities of the National Park are areas of limestone with so-called "clint and grike" patterns, caused when rainfall erodes weaker fissures, leaving high narrow ridges or overhangs of stronger rock. Ancient glaciers eroded many of the valleys, creating space for

the lakes as they melted at the end of the last Ice Age, approximately 8,000 B.C. Even today wind and water are still hard at work, gradually but continually changing the landscape.

These various types of geological formations and activities have created a multitude of environments. There are bare volcanic crags soaring from deep valley bottoms, spectacular waterfalls, high plateaus, and ridged fells with bracken (thickets of ferns and shrubs) and heather. Throughout the entire region, high ground breaks up areas of rolling meadows and verdant pasture. Deep valleys with babbling brooks and wooded copses give shelter to the small Lakeland communities. Today, thousands of kilometers of public footpaths and bridle ways extend to almost every valley and reach to every peak, offering new delights at every turn in the road.

The Lake District is rich in mineral deposits that have been put to good use since ancient times, and throughout much of the region's history, mining was a major industry. The iron-ore mine at Millom, on the coast southwest of Broughton-in-Furness, was once one of the biggest in the world. Farming has been another mainstay of the Lake District economy for centuries. To provide grazing land for

Hiking along Kirkland Pass is easier than it looks, and provides plenty of views.

9

sheep, which were raised for both wool and meat, large tracts of the forest that originally blanketed the whole area were cleared. Today, the sheep on the hillsides and in the vales define the region as much as do the fells and the lakes. The herds give a sense of proportion to the vast openness, just as the scattered farmhouses and characteristic drystone walls add reassuring warmth to even the loneliest valley. This is not an artificial landscape supported solely by tourism; today's working farms help keep the Lake District vital and distinctive.

Throughout history, the natives of this region carried on life in relative isolation from the rest of the country. The steep fells protected the population but also made transportation of any kind difficult; many of today's footpaths follow ancient pack-horse trails, which for centuries were the principal method of transport. Even today it is easy to see why major roads bypass the area; the only routes that traverse the region are smaller roads that twist and turn along the river dales and up through the craggy mountain passes. For many locals, a trip to the nearest market town would have been the farthest they would travel in a lifetime.

Not surprisingly, this self-contained region engendered a stalwart sense of self-reliance and independence in its inhabitants. When families live together for generations in the same town and valley, especially when these communities have been forced to pull together in times of hardship, a strong feeling of community is created, as has been the case throughout the history of this rugged territory. The traditional celebrations of rural life and the village sports days still give all members of local communities the chance to put their skills to the test and to enjoy each other's company. Favorite Lake District competitions range from wrestling and sheep dog trials to jam and cake making.

Life in the Lakes is still organized by the seasons and the activities of lambing, shearing, taking goods to market, and overwintering (the local farmers' term for "surviving the winter"). Seasons of plenty alternate with leaner periods when the people prepare to "mend and make do." Even today, when agricultural policies provide significant aid and resources, farming is still a tough life. There's little time for recreation in this sometimes harsh environment, and though local residents may come across as pragmatic and single-minded, you'll find them in a more relaxed mood at the end of a hard day's work, enjoying a pint of beer and game of dominoes at the local pub. The farmer you see standing over his crook at the side of the road may not give you a wide smile of welcome, but that short nod of his head and tip of his cap is equivalent to a heartfelt hug or handshake in other places.

Much of the farmland and many of the peaks and lakes are protected. This happened in response to attempts on the part of 19th-century industrialists and businessmen to exploit the area's natural resources. One plan in particular—a proposal to send a railway line through the heart of the region—galvanized a small group of influential local men, including poet William Wordsworth, into action. They succeeded in stopping the rail line at Windermere.

Sheep shearing time at Lakeland Sheep and Wool Centre in Cockermouth.

The natural beauty immortalized by Wordsworth's verses is still very much alive.

Since its founding in 1895, the National Trust has preserved nearly 100 farmhouses and the surrounding land as well as many other historic structures throughout the region. In 1951, the Lake District National Park was created, which extended this protection to a much wider area while imposing planning regulations and environmental guidelines and allowing further public access to the land.

Reacting in part to the effects of the Industrial Revolution, a group of 19th-century writers, known collectively as the "Lake Poets," did much to raise England's national consciousness about the landscape and natural beauties of the Lake District. City dwellers from northern England began to spend their free time here, walking on the fells or enjoying boat trips on the lakes. Their numbers have grown steadily ever since, and today many thousands of visitors come to enjoy the countryside and to visit the sites first made famous by Romantic poets. Tourism is now the biggest industry in the Lake District. Hotels, restaurants, and shops have proliferated, extending a warm welcome and the best of Lakeland hospitality to ever-growing numbers of visitors.

This popularity is also a source of considerable concern to many residents of the Lake District. Traffic jams, overflowing car parks, and eroded footpaths are all difficulties that need to be addressed. The challenge is how to stop the landscape from being changed by the very people who come to marvel at it. The National Trust and the National Park Authority both work on conservation projects and these, along with innovative transportation policies devised by local councils, are all designed to help minimize the potential negative impact of tourism.

Aside from these difficulties, which are suffered by National Parks all over the world, there is one other matter that can't be overlooked: rain. It rains regularly, whatever the season, so be prepared to experience some inclement weather during your visit. The rain irrigates the forests and fills the streams, waterfalls, and rivers that feed the lakes, so without it, of course, the magnificent landscapes would be altered forever. Fortunately, the Lake District retains its beauty in all types of weather, and in all seasons. Spring offers the fresh green of grasses in the valley and bracken on the hills. Woodland floors are blanketed with swathes of bluebells, and Gowbarrow Park, immortalized by Wordsworth, has its "host of golden daffodils." At lambing time, the frolicking youngsters are enchanting. Summer boasts long, warm days with strong sunlight and hazy views. Butterflies play among the blooms as day-trippers enjoy a picnic or a lakeside walk. Autumn brings the finest hues to the landscape, when the leaves turn shades of apricot and copper, the bracken changes to a burnt umber, and the hillsides glow in the low sunlight, reflecting perfectly in the glassy stillness of the lakes. After the first snowfall of winter, the fell tops turn white, complementing the walls of the rugged farmhouses and the gentle plumes of smoke that rise from log fires into the crisp cold air.

Recognized by a few individuals as a very precious resource, the Lake District has been praised in prose and verse and protected by wise policies so that the rest of the world can come and enjoy its particular beauty. No one who comes here can fail to be awed by the landscape and charmed by the lifestyle of this small yet spectacular corner of England.

A BRIEF HISTORY

Early History

Humans have been active in the Lake District for at least 8,000 years. The once densely forested fells and valleys were a safe and bountiful territory for prehistoric hunter-gatherers, and later, around 2500 B.C., after the forests had receded due to changes in weather patterns, settlers used the clearings in the lowlands for small-scale farming. The mysterious stone circles that dot the landscape are thought to be primitive calendars that helped the inhabitants decide when to plant and when to harvest. Castlerigg near Keswick is the best example. During the Stone Age, these early farmers devised ways to make axes and other tools from the harder rocks in the area, and as time passed, permanent settlements began to be established in this sheltered backwater.

Roman Influence

The Romans occupied this region in the first century A.D., but there is very little evidence to show that they actually conquered it. They built only a few settlements and roads in this part of Britain, which was very near the northernmost reach of their empire. Sturdy forts protected the mountain passes, and though the remains of a bathhouse at Ravenglass suggest that creature comforts weren't entirely lacking, life for the average Roman soldier was fairly harsh. A trip to remote Hardknott Fort, which protected the route through Eskdale and Hardknott Pass, provides a stark impression of what the invaders from the south were up against. Although the Romans stayed in Britain until A.D. 400, Hardknott, or Mediobogdum as it was known in those days, had been abandoned as early as the end of the second century. Whether the northern tribes made the pass diffi-

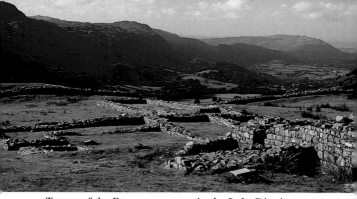

Traces of the Roman presence in the Lake District are most prominent at the ancient Hardknott Fort.

cult to defend by their constant raiding is still debated by scholars, but it is known that the local inhabitants weren't willing to give the Romans free rein over the whole territory. Even after Hadrian's Wall was built in the second century A.D., marauding bands from the north figured out a way to circumvent this formidable line of defense by launching their boats across the Solway Firth, landing on the coast of Cumbria south of the Wall, and attacking the Romans from behind.

The Celts and Christianity

The Celts arrived in the wake of the Roman withdrawal at the end of the fourth century. During the fifth century a number of Celtic tribes came together to form the Kingdom of Rheged, which is said to have stretched north over what is now the Scottish border and south as far as the River Mersey. Little is known about the kingdom, though it is documented that at this time the Celtic monks St. Kentigern and St. Herbert introduced Christianity to the region. Place names attest to the

Historical Landmarks

2500 B.C.   Development of agriculture and mining.

1st century A.D. Romans invade Britain.

4th century   The Roman Empire collapses; the Celts establish settlements.

5th century   Celtic tribes establish Kingdom of Rheged. Christianity introduced to the region.

1066   Norman forces conquer Britain; the Catholic Church becomes rich landowner.

1536   Henry VIII establishes the Church of England; Catholic monasteries dissolved.

16th century   Rise of the statesmen, or yeomen, farmers.

1770   William Wordsworth born.

1775   Thomas Gray writes *Journal in the Lakes*, the first guidebook to the region.

1835   Wordsworth's *Guide to the Lakes* a bestseller.

1847   Proposed railway line to Windermere and Ambleside creates a storm of protest.

1850   William Wordsworth dies.

1872   John Ruskin buys Brantwood.

1883   Lake District Defense Association founded.

1895   The National Trust is founded.

1905   Beatrix Potter buys Hill Top Farm.

1919   The Forestry Commission is founded.

1943   Beatrix Potter dies, leaving her land to the National Trust.

1951   Lake District National Park is established.

1974   Reorganization of local government leads to the creation of the county of Cumbria.

Celtic influence at every turn. It was a Welsh Celtic tribe that named the northern stretches of this territory "Cumbria" (the area was officially known as Cumberland until 1974). Penrith and Blencathra are also Celtic names, established during this early period of settlement. Later, in the seventh century, Anglian Christians moved in from the east and took over much of the land; from that point up until the tenth century the Lakelands were ruled from neighboring Northumbria. The Angles settled in the eastern lowlands, pushing the Celts onto higher and less fertile ground and west toward the coast.

Viking and Norman Conquests

In the early tenth century Viking raiding parties from Scandinavia began skirmishing with the Celtic tribes along the coast. Eventually, however, the warring gave way to Viking settlement and intermarriage with the Celts. The two races coexisted in the higher valleys, clearing tracts of land and establishing small villages. It is Viking vocabulary used today to describe many of the features of the landscape: *fell* (highland plateau), *tarn* (small lake), and *force* (waterfall) are all words from Scandinavian languages. The Vikings also left a legacy in unusual place names, such as Ullswater and Patterdale. Large stone crosses at Gosforth and Irton are two of the few physical remnants of their presence here.

The defeat of English forces at the Battle of Hastings in 1066 enabled the Norman forces of France to assume royal power. Life changed fundamentally: vast tracts of land were given to Norman lords and Roman Catholic religious orders. The monasteries and priories—including the very powerful abbey at Furness—assumed total control over all activities, and the residents became serfs to these new landlords. This new form of economic management changed the landscape of the Lake District once and for all. Climate changes had

Pele towers, constructed for protection against invading Scottish clans, can still be seen at Muncaster Castle.

already had the effect of reducing the amount of forest land; the monks accelerated this process by clearing many more acres in order to make room for ever-growing herds of sheep. This growth in animal husbandry led to the extinction of many of the non-domesticated animals that had roamed the countryside; numerous species, including the wild boar, died out by end of the 13th century.

Although remote from larger urban centers, the Lakeland area did not escape the Black Death, suffering three outbreaks in the mid-14th century. At the same time, marauding Scottish clans began to attack the Lakes. The border between England and Scotland was disputed, and the area was a constant battleground. English defeat at Bannockburn in 1314 heightened the tension. Kendal became a frontier castle, and pele towers—square defensive structures, from the word *pel,* meaning stake—were attached to the larger houses in the Lakes were to provide additional protection. You can still see these towers at Muncaster Castle and Dalemain. The defeat of the Scots at Flodden in 1513 finally turned the tables, and the pressure on the Lakes decreased.

Tudor Upheaval and the Statesmen

In the middle of the 16th century, the whole of England underwent a period of great turmoil. In 1536 King Henry VIII broke away from the Roman Catholic Church and declared himself head of a new Protestant faith, the Church of England. The great Catholic abbeys and priories, which had been the backbone of the economy, were destroyed by Henry's troops; social organization was replaced with terror and confusion.

The monetary wealth and vast tracts of land owned by the monasteries were redistributed according to Henry's favor. Many of the men who benefited were absentee landlords who needed people to manage the land for them. This resulted in the emergence of a new class of so-called "statesmen" or yeomen farmers, who came to comprise a new middle class. These permanent tenants paid rent to the landowner and made all the important decisions about the use of the land. As a class they came to even greater power and wealth by organizing trade and controlling the flow of goods in the area. Many were eventually able to buy the land they had been farming, and over time grand manors came to replace the more humble farmhouses earlier generations of yeomen had occupied. It was these statesmen who created a relatively secure micro-economy for the Lakes region, an economy based on agriculture and small-scale industry such as the production of textiles, bobbins, and charcoal.

The Industrial Revolution

The yeoman, or statesman, economy thrived for some 300 years, but with the rise in automation brought by the Industrial Revolution in the late 18th century, the demand for hand-crafted goods such as cloth plummeted—machine-produced goods were more plentiful and considerably less expensive. And in another shift in the economy, it was found that lamb could be raised more cost-effectively on lowland farms—in part because of the richer, more nutritious grazing land available there—and as a result Lakeland farms became less profitable. New roads brought competition from outside the area, which broke the local monopoly of the statesmen. The population of the Lakes region began to decline as people left to find a better life in the new industrial centers such as Manchester and Liverpool. Only Keswick thrived, primarily because of the pencil industry, for which it was world-famous.

The legendary pencil industry of Keswick is celebrated at the Cumberland Pencil Museum.

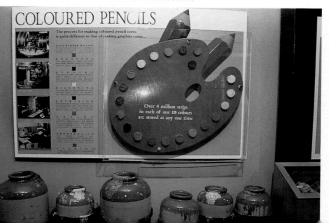

Writers and the Victorian Tourist Invasion

At the same time that the Industrial Revolution was wreaking havoc, however, a small but influential group of writers and poets settled in the area and began to write about its natural beauties and its lifestyle. William Wordsworth, the most famous of the group, was a local man, born in Cockermouth. He encouraged many in his literary circle to experience the beauty and peace of his native landscape, and as result of his efforts, its fame began to spread.

The improvements in roads and means of transportation that had in part been responsible for the decline of the yeoman economy now made it possible for more visitors to view the natural beauty of the Lakes region. Many of the high pack-horse routes had ceased to be used for the transportation of goods, but these old "rights of way" for foot and bridle traffic were now transformed into an extensive network of marked and mapped routes ideal for recreational walkers and hikers.

Preservation and Conservation

In 1857 the Great Western Railway Company built a main line to Scotland, skirting the Lakes on its way north. Some years later it submitted plans to expand the line into the heart of the region in order to link the towns of Windermere, Ambleside, Grasmere, and Keswick. This appalled Wordsworth, who said that the Lake District should be viewed as "a sort of national property, in which every man has a right and interest who has an eye to perceive and a heart to enjoy." After much debate, a line that terminated at Windermere and spared the rest of the Lake District was completed. Windermere and nearby Bowness became major resort towns. Then in 1879 the Manchester Corporation obtained permission to create a reservoir at the site of the Thirlmere lake. Outraged at the threatened loss of a beautiful natural valley, a group of concerned individuals formed the Lake District Defense Association to protect the lakes environment from further destruction and to oppose commercial exploitation. This organization was the precursor to the National Trust, which was founded in 1895 to "hold places of national interest and natural beauty for the benefit of the nation." It didn't win every battle, but assisted by high-profile friends such as Beatrix Potter, the National Trust slowly came to exert more influence. It now owns a number of important areas in the Lakes and many hundreds of historic sites all over the UK. As the main industries of the region continued to decline, the number of visitors continued to grow; it seemed that tourism could at least breath some life back into the region.

The Pressure of Popularity

Since the National Trust was founded, the area has benefited from increasing protection. The Forestry Commission, set up in 1919, is responsible for areas like Grizedale Forest. The Lake District National Park was created in 1951 to preserve the entire landscape and allow public access to areas of natural beauty. Throughout this time, the number of visitors has continued to grow, as has the volume of motor traffic. While the Lake District encourages and welcomes visitors, its popularity can damage the landscape and tax local transportation services.

In 1974 a total reorganization of local government throughout the UK did away with the old counties of Cumberland and Westmoreland and created the larger county of Cumbria. Today, the National Park Authority and the National Trust work with the Cumbria County Council and professional bodies like the Lake District Tourism and Conservation Partnership to formulate sensible plans for the future. Traffic and transportation policies are coordinated to

Walkers enjoy the tranquil beauty of Grizedale Forest, which features 75 sculptures.

alleviate bottlenecks, and footpath preservation allows continued access to the fells and remote valleys. All of these efforts are aimed at balancing the needs of the land, the farmers, and the visitors, ensuring that the Lake District remains a beautiful, natural place with many secrets to be discovered.

Famous People

William Wordsworth *(1770–1850):* Born in Cockermouth, Wordsworth was a true son of the Lakes. Chiefly known for his poetry, he had an earnest devotion to "plain living and high thinking." Senior member of the group known as the "Lake Poets," he became the chief exponent of the Romantic school of poetry, which was a response to societal changes brought about by the Industrial Revolution. Wordsworth sought to live in harmony with his surroundings and drew inspiration for his poetry from simple everyday actions and thoughts. He was, however, also interested in world affairs and gathered a circle of like-minded thinkers around him. Wordsworth's theories on man and society were highly regarded, and he campaigned hard to prevent modern encroachments like railway lines from damaging the Lake District. He was offered the title of poet laureate many times, but repeatedly declined because he didn't want to "work to order." At the age of 73, however, on the occasion of the death of his friend Robert Southey, he finally accepted the honor. He remained England's poet laureate until his death, though he never wrote a piece of official poetry.

Samuel Taylor Coleridge *(1772–1834):* Wordsworth's greatest friend, Coleridge is best remembered for his *Rime of the Ancient Mariner*. He and Wordsworth settled down in the Lake District at the same time, at the end of the 18th century. Coleridge's residence was at Greta Hall in Keswick. His time in the Lakes was less fortunate than Wordsworth's, however. Coleridge's marriage ended, his inspiration deserted him, and he slipped into depression and opium addiction. He left the Lakes in 1803, but the legacy of his work with Wordsworth (they collaborated on the *Lyrical Ballads*) makes him a favored son.

Robert Southey *(1774–1843):* Brother-in-law of Coleridge, Southey has to a certain extent been overshadowed by the legacy of Wordsworth and his circle, but in his time he was equally well regarded. He was extremely prolific, responsible for some 14,000 manuscripts ranging from poetry and prose to a history of Brazil to *The Three Bears*, a children's story. He was named poet laureate in 1813. After Coleridge departed from Keswick, Southey lived at Greta Hall until his death. In his later years he and Wordsworth formed a close friendship.

Thomas de Quincey *(1785–1859):* A writer, critic, and great admirer of Wordsworth, he took over the tenancy of Dove Cottage after his mentor moved to a larger house in Grasmere. He is best remembered for his book *Confessions of an English Opium Eater*, published in 1821. Unfortunately, de Quincey himself succumbed to addiction while living at the cottage.

John Ruskin *(1819–1900):* Highly accomplished in fields ranging from the arts to philosophy, education to environmental studies, Ruskin was one of the major figures of the Victorian Age, a social revolutionary who foresaw many of the problems of modern society. A tireless essayist, critic, and reformer, he wrote major critiques of the moral philosophies of the industrial age. His prodigious output and constant activity—including ambitious lecture tours—eventually brought him to the point of nervous exhaustion and resulted in the loss of his health and mental capacity.

Beatrix Potter *(1866–1943):* The author of *Tales of Peter Rabbit* was born in London but visited the Lake District every summer with her parents, falling in love with the region's landscape and wildlife. The royalties she earned from her first book allowed her to buy Hill Top, the tiny farm in Near Sawrey (outside of Windermere), and with the success of the many sequels she was able to buy several other tracts of land. After her marriage to solicitor William Heelis she wrote fewer books, concentrating instead on domestic affairs and farming; she was particularly devoted to breeding Herdwick sheep, which were in danger of disappearing from the countryside. At the end of her life she owned nine farms and many acres of land, all of which she bequeathed to the National Trust, on the condition that only Herdwick sheep be allowed to graze on it.

WHERE TO GO

THE SOUTHEAST

A land of rolling hills and deciduous trees, tiny hamlets and green meadows, the Southeast is the most popular area of the Lake District, if not the most dramatic visually. (You'll have to go farther north to reach the rugged fell landscapes.) The reputation of this area was guaranteed when the Victorian railway was built. Workers from the cities in northern England came to enjoy the fresh air, and rich industrialists built large lakeside houses surrounded by pleasant landscaped gardens. Many of these manors have now been converted into hotels known for comfortable accommodations and stunning views.

☞ Lake Windermere

The largest of the lakes at 17 km (10 miles) north to south, Lake Windermere has always been the most accessible, and therefore, not surprisingly, it is now the most developed. During the summer you will have to share the shoreline with many thousands of other visitors. Ferry services plying the lake provide one of the best ways to view coastline and the thickly wooded hills above. Boats are available for rent, and water-skiing and powerboat racing are very popular pastimes.

> You may be addressed as "love" as in "Thanks, love." This is simply a colloquial pleasantry used when names are not needed or known and when formalities seem unnecessary.

Among the several islands of interest on the lake is **Belle Isle**, still privately owned by the Curwen family, descendants of Fletcher Christian, of *Mutiny on the Bounty* fame, who was born near Cockermouth. It is said that after the crew of the *Bounty* settled on Pitcairn Island, Fletcher somehow

Rare moment of quietude at the launch of Lake Windermere, the Lake District's largest, most accessible body of water.

found his way back to England, living out his life on Belle Isle, protected by his family. Several local residents are said to have caught a glimpse of him but there is no firm evidence to support this claim.

Bowness and Windermere

Originally separate settlements, these two towns have now merged to the point that visitors can't tell where one starts and the other finishes. Genteel Windermere is more modern, having grown up around the railway station after the line was opened in 1847. If you travel by train to the Lakes, this is where you will arrive. Just around the corner from the station is the Tourist Information Centre, which will supply all the information you need about touring, accommodations, and restaurants. The town has a number of art galleries and many fine period hotels, and although it has few attractions it is a good base for trips farther afield in the Lakes.

Bowness began as small fishing village on the lakeside, but today it is a resort. It's still modest in size, but it becomes full to the brim on summer weekends, when families head here for fresh air. The town has many hotels and a number of shops where you can buy souvenirs or outdoor clothing.

Everyone seems to congregate around the lake's edge, where feeding the ducks and swans is a popular pastime. This is where the cruise boats dock. The ticket kiosks are right next to the wooden berths. You can take a lake tour or a ferry trip to Ambleside in the north or Lakeside in the south.

In the center of Bowness is the **Old Laundry Visitor Centre**; the theater housed here offers a program of performances throughout the year. Next door to the theater is **The World of Beatrix Potter**, an exhibition that provides a comprehensive introduction to the woman and her work. The presentation begins with a short video about the Potter stories and how they relate to the Lake District landscape. A delightful series of dioramas then introduce Peter Rabbit, Mrs. Tiggi-Winkle, and Squirrel Nutkin, among others, set in scenes taken from Potter's

Peter Rabbit remains one of Windermere's most renowned and celebrated native sons.

books. Another longer video relates to the life of Potter and her transformation from writer and illustrator (she did the original drawings for the books) to farmer, solicitor's wife, and early eco-warrior.

North of the town, **Windermere Steamboat Museum** looks back to the golden age of lake transport. A number of steamboats dating from the Victorian age until the 1920's are on display, all lovingly restored. Pride of place goes to *SL Dolly,* the oldest mechanically powered boat in the world (c. 1850), which was restored after spending over 60 years at the bottom of Lake Windermere. Weather permitting, you can take a ride on one of the steamers.

At Brockhole, about 2 km (3 miles) northwest of Windermere along the lake shore, is the **Lake District National Park Visitor Centre**, a very good place to gather information and plan your strategy for exploring. An audio-visual show gives information not only about the National Park but also about the work the staff does to protect the landscape. The mansion that now houses the Visitor Centre was once a private residence. Built in 1900, it reflects the Arts and Crafts style that was fashionable at the time. Surrounding the Centre are beautiful gardens with trails that lead through woodland and along the lake shore. There are places to relax or enjoy a picnic, and adventure playgrounds for the children. Special events such as pet shows, dog trials, and historical theme days are held throughout the summer.

Ambleside

Just a few kilometers north of Brockhole, at the northern tip of Lake Windermere, Ambleside is one of the major towns of the region. At the height of the summer season you'll share the town with many thousands of people, all jostling to stay on the narrow sidewalks. In the Victorian era, the town expanded northward from its original site (a Roman settlement at Waterhead); the commercial center now lies approximately 1 km (½ mile) from the lake.

Waterhead, Ambleside's harbor, has a few shops that cater to the ferries, cruise boats, and other vessels that dock here. There's a Tourist Information Centre in the main car park (open summer only). You'll find the remains of the Roman fort Galava a little way to the north, at the confluence of the Brathay and

---

Lake District Highlights

Lake cruises: on Windermere, Derwent Water, or Ullswater.

Dove Cottage, Grasmere, and Rydal Mount, Rydal Water. Homes of poet William Wordsworth and his family.

Hill Top, Near Sawrey. Farm owned by author Beatrix Potter.

Brockhole. Learn about the Lake District National Park.

Brantwood, Coniston Water. Home of author, artist and social theorist John Ruskin.

Hawkshead. Pretty village with many historic buildings.

Buttermere. Beautiful small lake with many gentle walks.

Town End Yeoman's Farmhouse, Troutbeck. Typical 17th-century farmhouse.

The Langdale Pikes. Dramatic fells and ancient volcanic peaks.

Hardknott and Wrynose Passes. Amazing road through awe-inspiring landscape.

Gowbarrow Park. In the spring the ground is carpeted with flowers, among them the daffodils that inspired Wordsworth. Among the best of English landscapes.

Aira Force. Beautiful waterfall within easy reach of the road.

Tarn Hows. Pretty tarn surrounded by woodland.

Ashness Bridge and Watendlath. One of the best-known views in the Lake District; a hidden valley of rugged hills.

Borrowdale. Dramatic valley with pretty villages.

Wast Water and Wasdale. Remote, magnificent landscape.

House over troubled waters: Bridge House spans the rushing Stock Ghyll in Ambleside.

Rothay, two of the rivers that feed Lake Windermere. Loughrigg, a low fell that gives spectacular views of both Windermere and Grasmere, is a short climb to the northwest.

Bridge House in Ambleside is one of the most popular sites and perhaps one of the most photographed buildings in the Lake District. Dating from the 17th century, it was a summer-house for Ambleside Hall, a large mansion built a century earlier, which, sadly, no longer exists. The tiny two-story slate house, which spans the bubbling waters of Stock Ghyll, now serves as a National Trust Information Centre and pick-up point for the National Trust tour bus. Across the main road from the house are several small streets that illustrate how the old town must have looked in the 17th century. Soak in the atmosphere as you wander down narrow alleys and cobbled lanes among white-washed cottages.

Stock Ghyll Force was one of the most popular visitor attractions during Victorian times. The 21-m (70-ft) waterfall was easily accessible from the town, even by ladies wearing the large heavy skirts of the time. Today people still take the same route to the force (sign-posted behind Barclays Bank in the town center) and to Stock Ghyll Water Mill. The **Armitt Library and Museum Centre**, just a little way beyond Bridge House, offers an interesting view on the life of the Lakes through the letters and books of local people. Founded by Mary Louisa Armitt in 1909, it provided a resource for scholars in the area; she donated her own collection of books, which encouraged others to follow suit. The library absorbed the Ambleside Book Club (Wordsworth had been its most famous member) and the Ruskin Library, which included many of Ruskin's private letters. Over the years the collection has grown to incorporate many objects and works of art, including a number of original scientific watercolors by Beatrix Potter, which show yet another facet of her talent. The collection is accessible via a hi-tech touch-screen directory.

Troutbeck

Sitting on the slopes of the Troutbeck Valley high above Bowness and Ambleside, Troutbeck is a tiny village of traditional farms and barns. The village is historically significant, and there are many fascinating architectural details to be found here. The most famous building in the village is the 17th-century **Town End Yeoman's Farmhouse**. A perfect example of a statesman farmer's house, this structure had been in the hands of the same family from the time it was built until it was taken over by the National Trust in 1947. There are two main rooms downstairs—the "firehouse," a utility area for washing and brewing, and the "downhouse," a living area with fireplace. The master bedroom is just off the downhouse; other members of the household slept in the loft. Town End is full of wonderful artifacts from 17th-century daily life, such as cooking utensils—bowls, pans, crockery, and hooks to hang hare and pheasants—rag rugs made by the women of the household, and laundry implements such as a "dolly" used for stirring the clothes in the washing tub.

Grasmere

Lake Grasmere (1½ km/1 mile long) and Grasmere village lie below a circle of rounded hills. Access to the lakeside is restricted, but the view from Loughrigg Terrace is one of the best in the Lake District and an easy walk from the village. **Rydal Water**, the smallest of the lakes in the entire Lake District, sits beside it; thousands of rushes line its banks. Grasmere village is one of the prettiest communities in the Lakes, but also one of the busiest. A settlement of stone cottages founded by Norse settlers, it became home to William Wordsworth and his sister Dorothy in 1799. The surrounding landscape, with drystone walls, farmhouses, and the Rothay river valley, became a source of inspiration for their artistic endeavors. **Dove Cottage** was their first home. Wordsworth loved the place and wrote some of his most memorable poetry while living here. The house has changed little since then; it has been faithfully preserved along with the garden the siblings faithfully tended.

Sara Nelson's Gingerbread Shop in Grasmere was once the village schoolroom.

Much of the furniture inside belonged to the family.

In 1802 William married Mary Hutchinson; the cottage became their family home. Eventually there wasn't enough space to house their children and their many visitors, so in 1808 the family moved to a larger home on the other side of the village. The Wordsworth Trust now manages the property and offers a guided tour of the cottage that provides insights into the life of the writer, his family, and his friends. Behind the cottage, the **Wordsworth Museum** displays many of Wordsworth's original manuscripts and other personal objects. Headphones allow you to listen to some of William's works while you view images of the landscapes that inspired him. The poet and many members of his family are buried in the graveyard of the **Parish Church of St. Oswald**, in the heart of Grasmere. The church itself is worthy of investigation. The structure dates from the 13th century, but a rather dull stucco finish was added in the 19th century. A rush-bearing ceremony (see page 93) is held here each August. At the corner of the churchyard is **Sara Nelson's Gingerbread Shop**, which is still making gingerbread and other goodies just as Sara herself once did for Victorian visitors who came to find Wordsworth's house. The tiny shop was once the village schoolroom, where children would sit with chalk and slate board.

The Wordsworth family made one more move, to **Rydal Mount** at the eastern tip of Rydal Water, and it was here that William lived for the last 37 years of his life. It is a much grander residence than Dove Cottage, yet it remains true to the poet's philosophy and world view—it's neither too imposing nor too lavish. Still owned by descendants of the poet, it is a family home rather than a museum, though it has been open to the public since 1970. There are many personal pieces and family portraits in the house, along with original Wordsworth manuscripts. The grounds are also very much as Wordsworth and Dorothy landscaped them, with four acres of sculptured lawn and a natural environment in which animals and birds thrive. The house has beautiful views of Lake Windermere, which must have brought the poet great pleasure in his later years.

The whole area around Grasmere and Rydal Water is full of gentle walks in beautiful deciduous woodland. For a wonderful walk that fills a whole day, try linking Grasmere village, Dove Cottage, and Rydal Mount. The route is 8 km (5 miles) long and includes some beautiful scenery. You could finish the trip with afternoon tea at Dove Cottage Teashop.

Inside the Life of Wordsworth

Wordsworth's poetry has been read and studied worldwide, but his sister Dorothy, who lived with him and his family throughout her life, kept a journal that paints a vivid picture of their everyday life. It is so detailed that we know that William liked gingerbread from the shop in Grasmere village. We can pinpoint exactly what he was doing when he was inspired to write his verse. Dorothy's journal is a sort of 18th-century "behind the scenes" documentary.

35

☞ Hawkshead

A village in miniature that is a delight to the eye, Hawkshead is comprised of whitewashed buildings huddled together around a tiny central square. The maze of narrow alleys that link the houses can be confusing, as there are few street signs to guide you, but the Tourist Information Centre provides an invaluable guide. Park in the main car park and walk the few meters into the village. There are many gems to be discovered: tiny leaded windows, gargoyles in the eaves, and flower-filled boxes on every window ledge.

The area was part of a huge tract of land owned by Furness Abbey, and the village produced cloth from their flocks, which went to market at Kendal. One of the oldest buildings, the Courthouse, was built in the 15th century. Just outside of Hawkshead, it is all that remains of the old manor house built by the monks of Furness, most of which was destroyed during the Reformation. The Courthouse now houses the **Museum of Rural Life**. From 1778 to 1787 Wordsworth was a pupil at the **Hawkshead Grammar School**, situated across from the Tourist Information Centre. The fledgling poet carved his name in one of the plain wooden desks, which proves that even a literary giant can once have been a naughty schoolboy. During this time he and his brothers lodged with Anne Tyson in a little house in the village.

The **Beatrix Potter Gallery** is housed in a tiny building on Main Street that was once the office of William Heelis, Potter's solicitor husband. Exhibiting a range of art works by the author, the gallery manages to convey a sense of the day-to-day life of Beatrix the author and illustrator and of her other life as Mrs. Heelis, wife and sheep farmer.

Two other notable buildings in Hawkshead are the **Quaker Meeting House**, dating from 1688, and the

Minstrel's Gallery Café on Flag Street, a 15th-century building that now provides refreshment for today's visitors.

In the hills northeast of Hawkshead is **Tarn Hows**. Created by the Marshall family (the original owners of the land) as a garden attraction, it has become one of the most popular sites in the Lake District. The family dammed the narrow valley and planted many of the lakeside trees. Beatrix Potter bought the tarn in 1929 and bequeathed it to the National Trust. Not just beautiful, it is a good place for those who enjoy a gentle stroll, popular with families and visitors with disabilities. The car park is barely 500 m (½ mile) from the tarn, and the footpaths around the water are wide, with gentle slopes.

Hill Top

Beatrix Potter's farm house and retreat is on the western shore of Lake Windermere at the village of Near Sawrey. The house was bought with the royalties she earned from her first book,

Many historic buildings stand in Hawkshead, including the Old Courthouse, now home of the Museum of Rural Life.

The Tales of Peter Rabbit. Potter received inspiration for many more characters from the animals in the village and surrounding farmland. The 17th-century cottage was her home from 1905; this was the place where she enjoyed the life of a lady farmer, tending her crops and breeding Herdwick sheep, a breed which was at that time waning in popularity but of which she was very fond. It is said that one of the conditions of her bequest to the National Trust was that Herdwick sheep must always be bred on her farms. The **Tower Bank Arms**, a pub that was featured in *The Tale of Gemima Puddleduck*, is very close to the cottage and a good place to stop for refreshment. Nearby is Esthwaite Water, a quiet lake that has a reputation for good trout fishing.

Grizedale

Grizedale is a forested area of nearly 12½ sq km (8 sq miles) between Lakes Windermere and Coniston. This ancient woodland of mixed deciduous and coniferous trees provided a source of fuel for the furnaces of the charcoal industry and the bobbin mills. Now under the control of the Forestry Commission, the forest has many kilometers of footpaths and cycle-ways to enjoy. **Grizedale Visitor and Wildlife Centre** has maps and information, particularly about the 75 sculptures visitors can find out in the woodland. These were all fashioned out of natural materials by local and international sculptors. The Gallery in the Forest, once the old sawmill, houses many other exhibits, and the Theatre in the Forest holds concerts and performances on weekends in the summer.

> The English have a special word for a two-week period, "fortnight," from the Old English meaning "fourteen nights."

South of Grizedale are a number of interesting attractions that you can reach by car or by lake ferry. Once at Lakeside on the southern shore of Lake Windermere, trains belonging to the

Lakeside and Haverthwaite Railway can take you on a pleasant 5-km (3½-mile) trip between Lakeside and the village of Haverthwaite. The thundering engine will transport you back to the age of steam. At the **Aquarium of the Lakes**, which is just beside the Lakeside Railway Station, you can familiarize yourself with the varieties of aquatic life that can be found around the National Park and beyond. Freshwater fish species swim in the tanks; there's also a seashore exhibit with a wave machine. More exotic exhibits include playful otters and a large seawater tank housing sharks and sting rays. It's an exciting

Grizedale Forest offers many opportunities for respite, such as this quiet winding road.

and well-planned aquarium, interesting whatever the weather but certainly a good place to spend a rainy afternoon. (You can buy a combination ticket for the railway and the aquarium.)

Over 60 bobbin mills once dotted the Windermere area. At Newby Mill near Lakeside Stott Park, **Bobbin Mill** was still operating commercially as recently as 1974. Twenty men once worked to produce turned goods for the wool mills, a market that eventually dried up when the wool industry went into decline. The steam engine that traditionally powered the plant was recommissioned in 1992 and is running three days a week. Guided tours through the mill, passing the leather belts that turn

A tour of the Stott Park bobbin mill illustrates the workings of this historic industry.

the shafts and over the wood shavings that scatter the floor, give an account of life at the mill during Victorian times.

Cartmel

Situated in the middle of the Cartmel peninsula south of Lake Windermere, the village of Cartmel has been at the heart of some important events in English history. In 1188 William Marshall gave land to build a priory at Cartmel, and during the Middle Ages it was a large and very wealthy concern. In his original covenant, Marshall stipulated that money would be available for the priory only if a part of the church were opened to the people of the surrounding countryside for worship. Thus, in effect, the priory's church became a parish church even though it was tended by a closed religious order. This clause became important at the time of the "dissolution," when Henry VIII destroyed other monasteries and priories. Cartmel church was saved only because it also served as a parish church for the community. Wander around the church (13th–15th century) to find some interesting artifacts of local history. Look for the plaque dedicated to William Myers, who, it says, died on 30 February 1762. There's also the so-called Vinegar Bible, dating from 1716. This volume shows a rare printer's error: in the story in the Gospel of John about Jesus

changing water into wine, the word "vineyard" was misprint-
ed as "vinegar." There is very little left of the actual priory—after it had been destroyed the stone was used to build the
village houses—but the Gate House remains intact. It has
been used over the centuries as a courthouse, a school, and a
village shop, and now houses a small museum.

Cartmel is a picturesque village, with winding streets and
fine houses. As you wander you may be surprised to find a
horse-racing track, and you may be even more surprised to
find no one is here: the track stays silent except for two race
meetings a year (late May and late August, on the long Bank
Holiday weekends). On these days the whole neighborhood
turns out and the tiny grandstand is full of people cheering.

A few kilometers to the southwest you'll find **Holker
Hall**, a historic house owned by Lord and Lady Cavendish.
It has beautiful landscaped gardens—it's said that the warm
air of the Gulf Stream aids in the production of the many
exotic blooms. The family offered their home as a refuge to
Queen Mary in the days after the abdication of her son
Edward VIII in 1936. She came here to escape the public
eye. (All this was in the days before the paparazzi, of
course.) The **Lakeland Motor Museum** on the grounds has
around 100 exhibits of various forms of vintage transport.
One wing of the house is open to the public, and the estate
also supports a 50-hectare (125-acre) deer park.

Kendal

The gateway to the Lakes for those traveling from the south,
this small sturdy town grew rich from trade in wool and cloth
that came from the central lakes. Kendal Green cloth was
famed throughout the land from the Middle Ages onward—it
was said to have been worn by Robin Hood. Kendal was the
first town in the area to receive a Market Charter in 1189,

which ensured its commercial prosperity. The town is still bustling today. The oldest sections are constrained within a one-way traffic system that gets clogged in summer but there are many surprises to be found if you take the time to wander the narrow streets. Look out for the **Chocolate Shop**, which first opened for business in 1657; the shop sells sumptuous and brightly wrapped treats, and the café on the upper floor serves unusual chocolate dishes and drinks.

The remains of historic **Kendal Castle** overlook the town. The Norman castle was the home of the Parr family, famous for having provided Henry VIII with his sixth and last wife, Catherine. She outlived him and returned to the castle after his death. The **Parish Church of Kendal**, built on land bequeathed to the church in Norman times, has the second widest nave in England. Next to it is Abbot Hall, a handsome Georgian Mansion that now houses the **Abbott Hall Art Gallery and Museum of Lakeland Life** complex. The main house, built in 1759, holds the largest collection of George Romney paintings in the country. Romney (1734–1802) was considered to be the third master of portraiture in the 18th century, alongside Thomas Gainsborough and Joshua Reynolds. Because of

Kendal Mint Cake

A hard confection with a mint flavor, which, before the revolution in isotonic drinks and dehydrated foods, was favored by walkers and mountaineers as a source of energy when they went on expedition. The bars are easy to carry and last for many weeks. Sir Edmund Hilary is said to have taken Kendal Mint Cake with him on his ascent of Everest.

The cake is not exclusively used by walkers: it is often served with coffee after dinner in Lake District hotels. You will find bars of the "cake" on sale in many shops in the area.

the gallery's high profile it attracts many important traveling exhibitions; check with the Tourist Information Centre about the current program. The Museum, situated in the renovated stable block of the house, has many dioramas of Lakeland life and industry from the last 200 years. It highlights the local craftsmen who helped Kendal and the other Lakes towns to thrive, and provides a comprehensive overview of how the economy of the Lakes has evolved and how the landscape has been changed by man.

Dioramas of historic scenes are on display at Kendal's Museum of Lakeland Life.

The **Kendal Museum of Archaeology and Natural History**, near the Railway Station, displays Neolithic and Roman finds from sites throughout the Lakes area, geological specimens, and a curious collection of stuffed animals from the region and throughout the world. Alfred Wainwright, prominent fell walker and writer, was curator here for many years. His guides with their maps and plans provide the classic companion to the high ground of the Lakes and his larger books make beautiful souvenirs. He died in 1990; his old office has been recreated in his memory.

Brewery Arts Centre, the home of community art in Kendal, offers classes, exhibitions, and performances, along with restaurants and coffee shops. The continually changing

Hours and Admissions

Abbot Hall Art Gallery. Abbot Hall, Kirkland, Kendal, Cumbria LA9 5AL. 15 Feb–31 Mar, 1 Nov–22 Dec, daily 10:30am–4pm; 1 Apr–31 Oct, daily 10:30am–5pm. Adult £2.80, child £1.25.

Beatrix Potter Gallery. Main Street, Hawkshead, Cumbria LA22 0NS. 1 Apr–1 Nov, Sun–Thur 10:30am–4:30pm (last admission 4pm). Adult £2.80, child £1.40.

Brockhole-Lake District National Park Visitors Centre. Windermere, Cumbria LA23 1LJ. 4 Apr–1 Nov, daily 10am–5pm. Free.

Dove Cottage and Wordsworth Museum. Town End, Grasmere, Cumbria LA22 9SH. Open 1–11 Jan, 9 Feb–31 Dec, (Closed 24–26 Dec) 9:30am–5:30pm (last admission 5pm). Adult £4.40, child £2.20.

Hill Top. Near Sawrey, Hawkshead, Cumbria LA22 0LF. 1 Apr–1 Nov, Wed–Sat, 11am–5pm (last admission 4:30pm). Adult £3.80, child £1.70.

Lake Cruises. Windermere, Coniston and Derwent Water offer cruises or ferry trips daily, 9am–dusk, weather permitting. Admission about £3–5 per trip. Ullswater cruises, 29 Mar–1 Nov, daily 10am–dusk. Adult £2.00, child £2.10. Steam Yacht Gondola, Pier Cottage, Coniston operates 1 Apr–1 Nov, daily. Adult £4.50, child £2.70.

Rydal Mount and Gardens. Ambleside, Cumbria LA22 9LU. 1–7 Jan, 2–28 Feb, 1 Nov–1 Dec, daily except Tue, 10am–4pm, 1 Mar–31 Oct, daily 9:30am–5pm (Closed 25 Dec). Adult £3.50, child £1.00.

Wordsworth House. Main Street, Cockermouth, Cumbria CA13 9RX. 1 Apr–30 Oct, Mon–Fri 11am–5pm. Adult £2.80, child £1.40.

World of Beatrix Potter. The Old Laundry, Crag Brow, Bowness-on-Windermere, Cumbria LA23 3BX. 28 Mar–30 Sept, daily, 10am–6:30pm; 1 Oct–31 Dec, daily, 10am–4pm. Adult £2.99, child £1.99.

program provides something for everyone, whether you want to join in or simply watch a master craftsman at work. The Centre sits just back from Highgate, on the same street with the Tourist Information Centre.

THE SOUTHWEST

The southwestern corner of the Lake District has some of the moodiest landscapes in all of the UK. Home to thousands of sheep and a few scattered farming families, the area is characterized by the stark beauty of bare peaks, rugged fells, and the most remote lakes, combined with challenging, narrow roads. You're sure to find a little remote spot all to yourself.

Coniston

Historically a center of copper mining and smelting, Coniston was a true working town and this heritage sets it apart from the other major towns in the Lakes. Less sophisticated than Ambleside and less commercial than Bowness, it has a simple charm that many visitors find more appealing. The remains of mining and quarrying sites on the face of **The Old Man of Coniston**, the mountain above the town, are a reminder of its history. John Ruskin, whose house sits on the eastern shore of Coniston Water, chose to be buried here, in the graveyard of the parish church, rather than in Westminster Abbey in London. The town in turn has honored him with a small museum.

Coniston Water

Coniston Water is long and narrow, the straightest of the Lake District lakes. It was this feature that attracted speedboat racer Donald Campbell. He'd had a series of victories in various types of powered vehicles, including a victory on land at Daytona Beach in Florida, before coming to Coniston in 1967 to attempt to break the world record in speed boating. His

The Victorian steamer "Gondola" is a pleasant means for passengers to enjoy the peaceful beauty of Lake Coniston.

efforts at Coniston ended in tragedy, however, as his boat left the water at high speed and broke into several pieces on shore. Campbell's body was never recovered.

Happier experiences were recorded by Arthur Ransom in his book *Swallows and Amazons* (1930). The lake and its islands were his inspiration for the story about the adventures of a group of children who are left to their own devices one summer in an age when innocence and security were taken for granted.

A pleasant way to enjoy the lake is to take a trip on the Victorian steamer *Gondola*. The National Trust runs the boat, which resembles the Venetian rowboats, and the plush interior takes one back to the genteel times when tourism was just in its infancy, when this steamer ride would have been just one part of a European "Grand Tour." The whole journey on this steamer takes about an hour.

One port of call for both *Gondola* and the other local boat service, Coniston Launch, is **Brantwood** on the eastern shoreline. This was the home of the 19th-century artist, critic, and reformer John Ruskin, one of the preeminent men of his time. Author of over 250 books and a prolific artist and art collector, he is perhaps best remembered as a social theorist; in this century many prominent figures, including Mahatma Gandhi, have been inspired by his writings. Ruskin lived at Brantwood from 1872 until his death in 1900, and in that time the house became a leading center of artistic and literary energy, much as Wordsworth's in Grasmere had just a few years before. Ruskin funded educational programs on the role of women in society and research into environmental pollution long before these issues became fashionable. Sadly, he became mentally unstable in his later life and died a broken man.

The house, which contains Ruskin's study and examples of his drawings and paintings, has magnificent views of the lake and the town of Coniston. The gardens, laid out by Ruskin himself, cover nearly one square kilometer (250 acres). Each year numerous exhibitions and open-air performances are held on the estate, and a commercial gallery on the grounds has an excellent selection of contemporary arts and crafts.

John Ruskin's bust is on view at Brantwood, where he spent his final years.

The Langdale Fells

If you have limited time in the Lake District and want to experience the high fells, do a little beginners-level hiking, or simply drive through some breathtaking countryside, then this is the place to visit. **The Great Langdale** and **Little Langdale** areas can be said to be the true heart of the Lake District, lying as they do in the very centre of the National Park. Interestingly enough, although possibly the best loved landscape in the Lake District for walkers and artists—Wordsworth described it as "unity, austere but reconciled,"—there is not a lake in sight. Their beauty and accessibility (being only a short drive from Ambleside) make them a must for all visitors.

The initial approach route, along the A593 from Ambleside, is characterized by rocky knolls rising from the valley bottoms. The River Brathay runs alongside the main road, carrying water from the fells that eventually flows into Lake Windermere. At Skelwith Bridge, turn right on to the B5343. The road leaves the valley floor and takes you past the small villages of Elterwater and Chapel Stile before offering the first real views of the Langdale Fells. The beautiful valleys and magnificent volcanic peaks—with such whimsical names as Harrison Stickle and Crinkle Crags—produce some of the finest vistas in the Lakes. No matter what the weather is like, the landscape is dramatic and breathtaking. If there is only one place where you get out of the car and do a little walking, this has to be it. Make a stop at Blea Tarn, only about a ten-minute walk from the car park; this beautiful body of water, surrounded by the high fells, offers one of the most beautiful views in the National Park. On a quiet day you'll feel as if you have the world to yourself.

From Blea Tarn the road drops sharply down to a T-junction, with signs right to Wrynose Pass. Take a left, towards

Sit back and relax—inside or out—with a pint of beer at the Brittania Inn pub in Elterwater.

the tiny village of Little Langdale. You will need to take care here, as there may be walkers on the road, especially at lunch time when everyone gathers in the village for a "pint" and a sandwich. Finally, once through the village of Colwith, you will reach the main road, the A593, and a right turn will lead you back to Ambleside.

Wrynose Pass and Hardknott Pass

West from Little Langdale toward the coast of the Irish Sea, there is only a single route—and it is one that tests the nerve of even the most experienced driver. The road climbs up through the tree line and into bracken fell (plateaus with thickets of shrubs) and sheep country until you reach the most difficult stretch of road in the Lake District, over the passes of Wrynose and Hardknott.

Wrynose Pass comes first: a single-track road with gradients of 1:4 will have you dodging sheep and other motorists around blind bends. As the road climbs, though, it offers spectacular views back to Little Langdale in the east; get out at the small car park at the top of the pass and take photographs. The Three Shires Stone at the roadside marks the meeting place of the historic shires of Lancashire, Cumberland, and Westmoreland. The road then drops down to Wrynose Bottom, a plain bereft of human life. The road shares the valley bottom with the Duddon River, flowing west to the sea. The fell has an eerie beauty about it; clouds frame the peaks here even on sunny days.

Hardknott Pass, with gradients of 1:3, is the mother of all Lakeland passes; the road is narrow and steep and twists like a switch-back ride. At the height of the season it can be choked with traffic and there are few passing places. It's a challenge, but many say that you haven't seen the Lakes unless you've traveled this road. Try it early in the day when there's much less traffic, or, if you really don't want to test your own driving skills, you can arrange for an organized tour with a driver; contact the Cumbria Tourist Board for more details (see page 125).

A Guide to Lakeland Words

The Lake District is beautiful, but the range of words used to describe its features can be confusing. Many are Norse or Old English in origin and have been used for many centuries. Here are a few to help you understand the landscape.

eck	stream	knott	rocky outcrop
dale	valley	mere	pond or lake
fell	hill	pike	sharp peak
force	waterfall	rigg	ridge
ghyll	watercourse/ravine	scar	escarpment
holme	island	tarn	small mountain lake

The **Hardknott Castle Roman Fort**, called Mediobogdum by its builders, sits on a shelf near the summit of the pass. The thick walls still clearly outline the fort's boundaries. Take a walk around the perimeter for breathtaking views of the valley below. Even on the warmest day a stiff, cold breeze blows steadily up the fell. Just imagine the kind of homesick letters a Roman-born legionnaire would have written back home.

Eskdale

Once you make it over the high point of Hardknott Pass, Eskdale opens up in front of you. It's almost like catching sight of Shangri-la: the vibrant green valley contrasts starkly with the rust-colored high ground. High drystone walls curb the narrow roads and rugged farmhouses nestle in the bottom of the valley. The tiny village of **Boot**, two hundred yards from the main road, is the first sign of civilization you'll encounter after coming over the passes. The two dozen or so houses—including some of the best self-catering lodgings in the Lakes—are clustered in a peaceful setting surrounded by the higher fells of Birker and Eskdale.

The **Eskdale Corn Mill** sits at the very top of the village, over Pack Horse Bridge. This 16th-century mill is still powered by the force of Whillan Beck, the water that comes racing down from the fells above. There are many sign-posted walks from Boot into the surrounding countryside, including a 3-km (2-mile) walk to the waterfalls of Stanley Force across the valley.

A little way along from Boot you'll find the terminus of the **Ravenglass and Eskdale Railway**, or "La'al Ratty," as it's affectionately known. A 38-cm (15-in) narrow-gauge railway, it carries a tiny engine and even smaller carriages through rolling countryside towards the coast at Ravenglass. Opened in 1875 to carry iron, it been operating as a recreational rail-

This isolated farmhouse is one of a dozen such beauties in the green valley of Eskdale.

way since 1960; a favorite with railroad enthusiasts, it runs all year round.

Wast Water

The deepest of all the lakes at 75 m (250 ft), Wast Water is bounded on the east side by steep slopes of gray scree (small loose stones) that tumble into the watery depths, and on the west by stretches of bracken. The lake itself lies in the shadow of several high mountains, including **Scafell Pike**, the highest in England at 977 m (3,205 ft).

This remote area is reached by a single long route from the central lakes, at the end of which you'll find the scattered buildings of the village of **Wasdale Head**. The rocks in this territory are volcanic and relatively young compared to the hills of the north. They have produced a stark and uncompromising landscape, with few trees breaking the lines of the mountain-tops. A total contrast to the pretty rolling hills of Derewentwater and Grasmere, it is a stark beauty, though no less alluring. On fine days the sunshine and shadows chase constantly across the water and rocky wastes, but stormy fronts that form in the Atlantic Ocean are caught by the mountain tops here, as a result of which they are almost always enveloped in clouds.

Wasdale, the birthplace of British fell-walking, is still very popular with experienced fell-walkers because its rocky crags give access to some of the most challenging hiking in the Lakes. Many who have their sights set on the Alps and Himalayas come to train on the peaks in this area. There are few easy walks on the higher ground, but around Wast Water and in the valley bottom you can enjoy footpaths that offer panoramic views of the mountains. The **Wasdale Head Inn** is a traditional meeting place, resting as it does in the lea of all the sheer ascents. You're bound to meet some hardy outdoor types in the bar.

A curious competition is held in Wasdale each November. The **"Biggest Liar in the World" Competition** is an amateur "story-telling" contest open to all comers. Fishermen and anglers seem to have the edge over most, but politicians and journalists are actually banned from taking part, since they are regarded as professionals.

Ravenglass

The Lake District National Park encompasses a short area of coastline where the tidal estuaries of the North Sea meet the streams and rivers flowing down from the western lakes. The main settlement on this coast is Ravenglass, a curious town of one main street with a hundred or so neat cottages huddled together against the prevailing winter winds. First settled by the Romans, it sits on a wide estuary created by the

Drystone Walling

One of the most distinguishing features of the fells and moors of Britain is the many kilometers of stone walls that meander along the valley floors and over the peaks. These walls are remarkable in that builders employ no mortar in their construction. It is simply the skill of the artisan, and his knowledge of the stones—their shape and their relationship to each other—that ensure the strength of the whole structure.

Full steam ahead! The narrow gauge Ravenglass Railway, built in 1875, was converted to recreational use in 1960.

confluence of three rivers. The Romans called their town Clanoventa ("the town on the bank"). All that remains of the original settlement are the ruins of a Roman bathhouse, just a little ways from today's town. Walk under the railway line and turn right down a farm track. This is the headquarters of the Ravenglass and Eskdale Railway—the little trains spend the night in the sidings here. The station has a bar and a collection of railway memorabilia.

The tidal estuary harbors a number of islands that serve as important breeding grounds for seabirds. It can be dangerous to explore the open, sandy areas on these islands since the tides rise very quickly; be sure to check the tidal tables before setting out.

Nearby is **Muncaster Castle**, a structure offering much in the way of English history. Built on Roman foundations, the castle was erected in the late 13th century to keep the Scots at bay—its strategic position affords good views of the surrounding lowland. Since the 13th century, the castle has been owned by the Pennington family, who feel that their tenancy is protected by the terms of an ancient royal gift. In 1464, after the Battle of Hexham, King Henry VI wandered the countryside and many of the landowners, unsure whether he was victor or vanquished, refused to give him shelter. Sir John Pennington, however, invited him into Muncaster. When Henry returned to his duties he gave his drinking bowl to the family, saying that as long as the cup remained unbroken the family would remain at Muncaster. Needless to say the bowl, which is still in one piece, is kept under lock and key at all times.

Over the generations the castle has been expanded, but it is still essentially a family home, full of furniture, books, and family portraits. Visitors can tour the house with a tape-recorded

The Countryside Code

This is a series of simple guidelines meant to enable visitors to natural areas to enjoy their stay while making minimal impact on the environment and the lives of those who live and work there. They are:

Guard against all risk of fire
Fasten all gates
Keep your dogs under close control
Keep to the public paths across farmland
Use gates and styles to cross fences, hedges, and walls
Leave livestock, crops, and machinery alone
Take your litter home
Help to keep all waters clean
Protect wildlife, plants, and trees
Take special care on country roads
Make no unnecessary noise

narrative that gives detailed information about each room. The 32 hectares (80 acres) of garden are equally pleasing. Rhododendrons and other exotic plants imported from China during the 19th century have created one of the finest gardens in northern England. The castle grounds are also home to **The Owl Centre**, a conservancy devoted to saving the 150 species of owl found around the world. Calling itself a "Noah's ark for owls," the Owl Centre hosts a bird flight event every afternoon at 2:30.

Muncaster Mill, 3 km (2 miles) north of the castle, started operating in 1455, although the present building dates from the 18th century. It is still used to grind oatmeal and whole-wheat flour, which is available for sale. The mill sits on the River Mite, and "La'al Ratty" makes a regular stop here.

Duddon Valley

The Duddon Valley and the rolling hillsides around the village of **Ulpha** were much favored by Wordsworth. He wrote "Sonnets on the River Duddon" in praise of the area. This is

> To avoid getting mud on carpets, people often take their dirty walking boots off at the entrances to pubs or hotels.

true moorland—open stretches of heath that contrast sharply with the high peaks in the background. The views of Scafell and the Cumbrian Mountains from the road that crosses Ulpha Fell (in the direction of Eskdale and Eskdale Green) are splendid. And if you really cannot face the excitement and exhilaration of crossing Wrynose and Hardknott passes, this road offers a far less taxing way to reach the coast and the far west of the Lakeland.

THE NORTHEAST

Boasting some of William Wordsworth's favorite haunts as well as an old Roman road that is now a very popular hiking

Muncaster Mill has been grinding oatmeal and flour since 1455. The present building dates from the 18th century.

route, the Northeast is spectacular walking country, transitional terrain between the Lake District's high fells and peaks and the lowland passes around Penrith and the Eden valley. These passes were used as a gateway to the Lake District by armies of marauding Scots. All of these passes and many kilometers of walking trails surround the region's single (though impressive) large lake—Ullswater. At the eastern reaches the high ground gives way to undulating farmland.

Kirkstone Pass

Leading northeast from Lake Windermere to Ullswater, Kirkstone Pass on the A592 is the highest in the Lakes—446 m (1,489 ft). The Kirkstone Inn, an old coach house and now local landmark, was built here to shelter travelers on the hazardous trip between Penrith and the central lakes area. Despite the high altitude, Kirkstone Pass is in fact the easiest of the Lake District passes to traverse, since the valley floor is very

The Aira Force waterfall is one of Ullswater's most alluring scenic spots.

wide, even at the highest level. Watch for a car park just beyond the summit, where you can stop and enjoy the awe-inspiring view north over the diminutive Brothers Water, so called because two brothers were said to have drowned in its depths.

The road then follows the valley bottom through the towns of **Patterdale** and **Glenridding**. Both towns, once centers for mining, are good starting points for walking, hiking, and pony trekking into the surrounding fells and mountains.

Ullswater

Ullswater is the one major lake in the northeast corner of the Lake District. At 12 km (7½ miles) in length, it is the second-largest lake after Windermere, but it does not have the commercial development of its big brother and is far less busy. The character of the lake changes as you travel along its length; the shape of the valley constantly alters the perspective, a fact that has not been overlooked by generations of painters and photographers. Many people visit the area to take advantage of the water sports; it is particularly popular with canoeists. Both Glenridding and Patterdale offer boat rentals. The road from Ambleside to Penrith (A592) runs along the length of the north shore. From here it is possible to stop and admire the view. Those who don't want to drive or walk around it can take the ferry, which travels down the whole length of the lake from Glenridding to Pooley Bridge.

Gowbarrow Park

Just beyond the turning for Dockray is Gowbarrow Park, which rolls across the hillside above Ullswater. This is the spot where Wordsworth's sister Dorothy was stopped in her tracks by what she believed were the most beautiful daffodils she had ever seen; her astonishment inspired Wordsworth to write about this "host of golden Daffodils" in one of the best-loved poems of the English language, "I Wandered Lonely as a Cloud" (1804). The park is at its very best in spring, when you can walk through a carpet of flowers surrounded by the fresh green leaves of the newly awakened woodland.

Here you'll also encounter one of the most popular water-falls in the Lake District. Beautiful at any time of year, **Aira Force** is a 20-m (60-ft) waterfall spanned at its peak by a narrow stone foot-bridge. It is a favorite subject for photog-raphers, in part because of the wonderful woodland setting with rare mosses and fantastic Monkey Puzzle trees. The car park from the A5091 offers the shortest route to the falls.

At the northern tip of Ullswater there is a right turn to **Pooley Bridge**, the northernmost stop for the lake steamer. The road leads farther along the eastern shore of the lake to **Martindale** with its pretty Elizabethan church, St. Martin. Though the road eventually reaches a dead end, there are a number of marked hiking routes back towards Ullswater or south over higher ground to Patterdale. About 3 km (2 miles) farther down the road is the **Sharrow Bay Hotel**, the first and arguably still the best country-house hotel in the Lake District. Try lunch or afternoon tea on the terrace.

Dalemain Country House

This distinguished house is remarkable for its longevity and conglomeration of architectural styles. Behind the fine Georgian façade, made of local sandstone, is a genuine Tudor structure (including the Fretwork Room, with its magnificent 16th-century oak paneling), a manor hall dating from 1400 (which now houses the restaurant/café), and a Norman pele tower. In the 12th century, when the house consisted of little more than the pele tower, it was owned by the de Morville family (one of the more infamous members of this family, Hugh de Morville, was one of the four knights who murdered Thomas á Becket in Canterbury Cathedral in 1170). Since 1679 it has been owned by the Hasell family, who built the Georgian extension, and who over the generations have carefully managed the treasures that fill the house. Visitors today can examine the traces of the house's complicated architectural legacy and explore such fascinating historical oddities as the "priest's hiding hole," built during the Reformation as an emergency escape route for Catholic priests who had been invited in to say Mass. Access to the chapel and the hiding hole was through the fireplace, which would be lit to help confound pursuers. There are also a number of museums in the magnificent grounds, including a Fell Pony Museum and the Yeoman's Museum.

Rheged

This attraction, an amazing adventure in an ancient kingdom opened during the summer of 1999, and offers a chance to take a journey through the history of Cumbria. There are displays, exhibitions, and a massive multi-screen cinema experience, complimented by speciality shops, restaurants, cafés, and an indoor play center. All this is in a fantastic five-story building in the middle of an old quarry.

The roof is covered in grass, making it the largest earth covered building in Britain.

Penrith

The gateway to the Lake District for those traveling from the north, Penrith was often at the center of battles between the English and the Scots for control of this frontier territory. The town center is a curious tangle of winding streets, laid out that way, some say, to confound enemies. The many little alleys, or "yards," as they're called, were used to protect herds of sheep brought down from the fells during times of crisis. Today it is a thriving market town, not yet in the full grip of the tourist boom. The lively cattle market makes Penrith a center for the economic activity of the area. The Tourist Information Centre and a small town museum are housed in a plain, sturdy building from Elizabethan times known as **Robinson's School**. Above the town, across from the railway station, are the

The Dalemain Country House stands majestically in the historic economic center of Penrith.

*Ancient recycling center—the walls of Penrith Castle were
dismantled and used to build other structures in the town.*

remains of **Penrith Castle**, built to protect against raids from
the north. Traditional home of the Neville family, the castle fell
into royal possession after a series of skirmishes. King Edward
IV granted the castle and land to Richard of Gloucester—who
later became King Richard III—and it stood as a bastion of the
English crown. Later, as it fell into disrepair, the walls were
dismantled and used to build other structures in the town. You
can see the characteristic red stone on almost every street.

Askham

South of Penrith is an area of farmland that forms the eastern
boundary of the National Park. With its wealth of pretty cottages, Askham is a true farming community. The long village
green is a wonderful place for a stroll, and an even better place
to take a break, thanks to number of good pubs. A little way
from Askham village is **Lowther Park**. This large estate once
centered on a fairy-tale castle, the remains of which can still

be seen from the outside (it's not open to the public). The vast grounds have been turned into a leisure park (open summer only) which has more than forty attractions. Set in grassland and rolling countryside is a deer park, a bird-of-prey attraction, a circus, and a theme park. There's lots for children to do, and there are some wonderful spaces for secluded picnics.

Haweswater

This windswept area of water is close to the central lakes as the crow flies, but it takes a long time to reach by car. Many people walk the distance, using **High Street**, the path of an old Roman road that cuts across the fell tops from Lake Windermere toward Penrith. Gentler footpaths radiate from it on to the vast commons of Brampton and Martindale, but the main part of this route is not for the inexperienced or the unfit.

The Haweswater that you see today is man-made. The 6½-km (4-mile) long reservoir was created in 1941. The road travels to the head of the reservoir, and footpaths lead through wonderful undulating countryside all around the lake and onto Mardale Common. The area gets crowded in summer, partly due to interest in the nesting golden eagles, which have been returned to the area because of the efforts of environmentalists. There are no facilities here, so bring food and drink with you.

Caldbeck

The northernmost village in the National Park and once a mining town, Caldbeck, with its pastel cottages on either side of Chalk Beck, is now rather sleepy. The only remaining evidence of industry is **Priests Mill**, which has been a corn mill, a bobbin mill, and a sawmill. The water wheel and sluice gate still operate in summer, and there is a small display of artifacts used over the years; the mill buildings themselves have been converted to a gift shop and café. In the churchyard of **St. Kentigern**

church, opposite the mill, is the grave of John Peel. A landowner and leader of the local hunt, Peel was a larger-than-life character, well known throughout the region in his day. One of his friends, the poet Robert Graves, wrote a poem about his antics. The verses were set to music in the mid-19th century and since then the song "D'ye Ken John Peel" have been taught in every English school. You will also find the grave of the "Beauty of Buttermere" nearby (see page 72).

THE NORTHWEST

With forests and fells, a valley of breathtaking beauty, and the most spectacular lake setting in the National Park, this area has a greater variety of views than any other in the Lake District.

Keswick

This town of sturdy Victorian houses made of gray Lakeland stone has a stunning setting, nestled as it is in a natural bowl on the shores of Derwentwater and surrounded by green hills. The biggest town in the National Park, the population of Keswick (pronounced "kezzick") swells each summer as hikers, boaters, and sightseers arrive. Keswick makes a good base for touring the National Park and the Northwest. A working town through much of its history,

A traditional clog maker practices his craft at a shop in sleepy Caldbeck.

with the wool and mining industries as major employers, Keswick also aroused the interest of writers and artists. Coleridge and Southey, two of the more prominent Lake Poets, both lived here and raised the profile of the town and the surrounding area. **Greta Hall**, once the home of Southey and his family and now part of Keswick School, is unfortunately not open to the public. **Moot Hall**, a slate structure built in the early 19th century and used for Church of England services when the community had no

Main Street, UK. Keswick makes a good base for exploring the National Park.

church, sits in the center of town surrounded by the bustle of small shops and, on Saturdays, market stalls. You will find the tourist information center here. Century Theatre offers a program of performances ranging from drama to Gilbert and Sullivan to English pantomime. Originally a traveling group, the company has found a permanent home in Keswick. The box office is next to the Tourist Information Centre.

The **Cumberland Pencil Factory**, a leading producer of pencils in the world, would appear to have little to offer the visitor, but the **Pencil Museum** provides fascinating insights into the history of pencil production in the area. It all began in the 15th century, when an important seam of graphite was found in neighboring Borrowdale. There are displays and videos, including excerpts of the famous video, *The Snowman,* which was produced—as were the original book illustrations—using

Cumberland's Derwent line of color pencils. Visitors also learn how Cumberland pencils helped some prisoners escape from Nazi Germany during World War II. When entering the museum, children are offered worksheets that keep them busy seeking out information from displays and diagrams; they seem to relish the challenge, as do many of the parents. At the back of the exhibit is an area set aside for activities such as drawing, brass rubbing, and finger painting.

The **Keswick Museum and Art Gallery** in Fitz Park is a treasure trove of artifacts collected in the area, with the atmosphere of an old professor's study. A collection of stuffed birds and preserved butterflies sits alongside rock samples and Stone Age axes. Perhaps the greatest collection is housed in the small Art Gallery. A series of neat wooden display cases hold manuscripts and personal articles of the luminaries of the Lakeland region—scripts from the hand of Robert Southey and letters written by Ruskin along with objects such as their tea cups, clogs, and purses.

Fitz Park itself is a fine example of the philanthropic attitude of the Victorians, who created green spaces in almost every town for the people to enjoy. Although many parks around the country have been allowed to fall into decay, Keswick has kept its park tidy and in good repair, with neat flower beds and pretty borders.

Castlerigg Stone Circle

Just above Keswick, sitting in the shadow of the mighty **Blencathra**, or "Saddleback," mountain to the north, is a late Neolithic/early Bronze Age circle of 48 stones. Its impressive setting on a rounded hill just below the high peaks and out of sight of modern buildings allows the visitor to gain an impression of times past, when the circle was used in ancient and mysterious rituals.

The Castlerigg Stone Circle—used in ancient, mysterious rituals—dates from the late Neolithic/early Bronze Age.

Derwent Water

Its wooded shores, delightful islands, and beautiful setting have earned Derwent Water the epithet "Queen of the Lakes." At just 5 km (3 miles) in length it is more manageable than some of the larger lakes. Surrounded by rounded fells rather than high mountains, the countryside here is restful rather than challenging, and the walking is easy. Footpaths along the water's edge lead to pretty wooden bridges and reed beds, which are home to a wealth of bird and water life. In the distance are Skiddaw Peak to the north and Cat Bells in the west.

Lakeside is just a five-minute walk from Keswick, via a footpath that leads along the shore line. This is where the Derwent Water ferry moors. The lake ferry provides a relaxing way to take in the beautiful setting and get a closer look at some of the islands. If you feel more energetic, you can rent a rowboat at the dock and set out under your own steam. **St. Herbert's Island** was named after the saint who lived here as a hermit; after his death in 687 it became a place of pilgrimage.

On the northwest shore of the lake is **Lingolm**, historic home of Lord Rochdale. Beatrix Potter spent many happy holidays here as a child with her parents, who were friends of Rochdale. It was during these holidays that her love of the Lake District was born. The house is famed for its gardens—particularly its rhododendrons, which were highly prized at the end of the 19th century—and its beautiful setting; from here you can marvel at panoramic views of the lake and Skiddaw Peak and Blenthcathra beyond.

The B5289 road, which runs south from Keswick along the eastern shore of Derwent Water, leads you to some of the best gems of the Lake District. It's worth taking a day's drive or a few days of walking to seek them out. After leaving Keswick, the road finds the lake's edge and leads you to wonderful views of Cat Bells peak on the western bank. Your eye will be drawn right, but be sure not to miss the left junction at the sign for Watendlath. Take this small road, which climbs up through wooded hillsides; about a kilometer (½ mile) from the main road is **Ashness Bridge**, a tiny stone bridge spanning a modest little beck. It's become very popular, though, because from it

Poet Laureate

"Poet Laureate" is an official position within the British Royal Household. The holder of the title—usually the most eminent poet of the day— receives a stipend and a mandate to write poetry for official state and other royal occasion. Robert Southey and William Wordsworth, two of the most prominent of the Lake Poets, both served as poet laureate in their time, though Wordsworth prided himself on not ever actually having written any "official" verses.

Queen of the Lakes — sailboats skirt across Derwent Water as Skiddaw Peak rises up in the background.

you can enjoy a splendid view of Derwent Water and the fells — it's an almost perfectly framed natural composition, something no photographer, professional or amateur, can resist.

A few kilometers farther south you'll come upon "**Surprise View**," a lookout that offers a panoramic vista of Derwent Water with Bassenthwaite Lake in the distance. It's an awe-inspiring sight, but beware of the sheer drop, especially on a windy day. As the road climbs higher you'll reach a hidden valley, left behind as the glaciers of the Ice Age melted. **Watendlath**, Norse for "the barn at the end of the water," is one of the best places to enjoy the stark fell landscape without much exertion. The walks lie along the stream bed on a plateau high above Derwent Water. The tiny village of Watendlath is beautiful — a small farming community beside a small tarn, set in a natural bowl surrounded by stark fells, it seems to lie far away from the 20th century. Travel over the 15th-century pack-horse bridge to

Sheep crossing—from Seatoller village begins the steep ascent up Honister Pass.

reach footpaths that lead to the surrounding valleys. It's difficult to believe that this little spot was once a major junction for traffic in the lakes before motorized vehicles were invented. For a wonderful afternoon walk of about 10 km (6 miles) you can leave your car at Ashness Bridge and walk up along the path of the beck to Watendlath.

Return to the B5289 and continue toward the southern tip of Derwent Water. In the Lodore area, it's worth taking a detour to see **Lodore Falls**, situated behind the Lodore Hotel. The impact that the falls make will depend to a certain extent on what kind of weather the area has been experiencing: after a spell of rain they're a spectacular torrent, but in dry weather the flow can slow to a mere trickle. Park in the Kettlewell car park, which is just beyond the Watendlath turn-off.

Borrowdale

The B5289 moves along the shores of Derwent Water and then follows the beautiful green valley of the River Derwent, where families gather to swim and picnic. This is Borrowdale, the most famous valley in the Lake District. The twin span bridge at Grange marks the start of the valley. Filled with deciduous woodland, green fields, small villages, and farmhouses, this is the epitome of northern English landscape.

Near the village of **Rosthwaite** is the **Bowder Stone**, a giant lump of rock left behind by glacial ice that receded at a very slow pace. It's said to weigh 2,000 tons (1.8 million kg/4 million pounds). Standing on a small, narrow base in a gully surrounded by trees, it looks like an upside-down iceberg. The stone was much loved by Victorian visitors, who would have their photographs taken with hands outstretched against the rock face, as if to show that they were strong enough to hold up the massive stone.

> **"Queuing" is still a British ritual. Be ready to "wait your turn."**

Just before the village of Seatoller is a junction with a sign for **Seathwaite**, said to be the wettest settlement in Britain. The rainfall recorded here is almost one third more than in nearby valleys; since the actual number of rainy days is no higher for Seathwaite, it's believed that it must be the setting of the village that accounts for the higher volume. Seathwaite is the gateway to **Scafell Pike** (a 6-km/4-mile footpath connects them), and the mountain may attract more clouds and more intense rain than other peaks in the lakes.

Seatoller village is home to the **Seatoller National Park Visitor Centre**. From here the road turns out of the Borrowdale valley to begin a steep ascent westward through Honister Pass. This is one of the most difficult passes to ascend, but also, arguably, the prettiest. Grey scree slopes dominate both sides of the pass, which only sheep seem to be able to move across with ease. The narrow view creates a tunnel effect—the eye is drawn directly ahead towards the peaks of High Stile and Red Pike, which cradle the lake and village of Buttermere.

Buttermere

Buttermere is one of the pearls of the Lake district. Small and accessible, it is possible to walk around its shoreline in a couple of hours. Most of the route is relatively flat and all of it is picturesque. The small copse planted here has created a photographer's delight. Water, hills, and trees combine to offer some of the most memorable views in the National Park. Buttermere Lake is one of the homes of Lake District char, relatives of the salmon that were trapped here by the changes in sea and land levels after the last Ice Age.

The tiny village of Buttermere has a number of restaurants and cafés that are good for lunch. It's a popular little spot, though, so there are usually problems with parking on all but the quietest weekends. The village was made famous in the 19th century, when a writer named J. Budworth encountered Mary Robinson, the beautiful daughter of the landlord of the Fish Inn. In his book *A Fortnight's Ramble in the Lakes* Budworth christened her the "Beauty of Buttermere." For years after the book was published, devoted (and curious) readers came from all around to see this beauty for themselves. Mary succumbed to all the attention and was swept off her feet by one these admirers, a certain Colonel Hope M.P. Despite his exalted station, the good Colonel turned out to be an imposter and a bigamist, and after their marriage

The Sheepdog

Every movement of a flock of sheep is determined by the skill of the farmer and his dog. Fell dogs need to be very disciplined and the Border Collie is the breed most often used. It is naturally highly intelligent and full of energy.

Lakeland farmers like to say that up to the age of three, the dog is an apprentice, by the age of six he works in partnership with the farmer, but by the age of nine he thinks he knows more than the farmer. Not surprisingly, retirement soon follows, to make way for a younger dog.

was sent to jail. But Mary managed to make a new life for herself with a local man, and gave birth to seven children. She is buried in Caldbeck (see page 63).

Just a little farther along the valley to the northwest, joined to Buttermere by a stream, lie two other lakes. **Crummock Water** lies in the shadow of dramatic **Mellbreak Peak**. From its western shore you can gain access to **Scale Force**, at 60 m (170 ft) the highest waterfall in the Lake District. It is 3 km (2 miles) to the falls by footpath from Buttermere village. **Loweswater** is the smallest of the three lakes and never crowded. With footpath access and picnic sites, it makes a restful place to spend an afternoon.

Bassenthwaite Lake

Bassenthwaite Lake, just under 6 km (4 miles) in length, lies to the northwest of Keswick. It proved to be an inspiration to Alfred Lord Tennyson when he was writing his poem "Morte d'Arthur." Tennyson's description of the lake into which an anguished Arthur throws his sword Excalibur is based on Bassenthwaite. At the time the poet was staying on the eastern shore at Mirehouse, the imposing family residence of his friend James Spedding. The house is now open to the public, with limited hours. Its large garden has a number of different environments, from a formal herb garden to open pasture land. On the grounds is the tiny **Church of St. Begas**, which is always left open for travelers. Public footpaths link the gardens with Dodd Woods and the peak of Skiddaw behind.

Bassenthwaite is not as frequently visited as some of the other lakes — there is no ferry service and water activities are restricted. It is well known by anglers, however, who value it for its good supplies of sport fish, such as char.

The village of Bassenthwaite spreads out across the valley to the north of the lake. **Trotters and Friends Animal Farm** was a working farm that now opens its doors to visitors and offers opportunities to feed, pet, and pick up the animals. Some of the creatures here are decidedly exotic—including lizards and snakes—but others are old Lakeland favorites, like Herdwich sheep and native cows and pigs that can be found all across the countryside. Animal feeding takes place every day during the summer and there are also tractor rides, weather permitting. With a café and picnic area, it's a great place for children of all ages.

Skiddaw

At 931 m (3054 ft) Skiddaw is one of the major peaks of the northern Lakeland area, and one of the three highest in England. Its rounded form testifies to the fact that it is also one of the oldest. The whole mountain was once blanketed in forest and designated as a royal hunting area. In the 19th century it was a favorite haunt of Coleridge and other English Romantics. It is the easiest of the big peaks to climb, but the effort will still take up an entire day. The car park near Ormathwaite is the best place to start. Or, for a somewhat easier ascent, you could try scaling **Latrigg**, another peak a few kilometers to the south, closer to Keswick. This climb offers panoramic views of Derwentwater and Borrowdale.

Whinlatter Pass

There are two roads to Cockermouth in the far northwest corner of the Lake District. The fast road travels the length of the eastern shore of Bassenthwaite Lake; the slower, and more picturesque, route leads through **Whinlatter Forest**. This dense pine forest looks spectacular against a blue summer sky, and there are picnic sites and trails through the trees. The Whinlatter Pass Visitor Centre is a hub for many cycle paths and walks.

Skiddaw skidaddle—hikers amble along a narrow road, with Skiddaw Peak gleaming in the distance behind them.

Cockermouth

A no-nonsense working town with a wide tree-lined main street and pastel painted houses, Cockermouth has an air of quiet gentility. There is still a regular cattle market here for the farmers from the surrounding countryside. The main attractions are linked to the town's most prominent son, William Wordsworth, who was born here in 1770. The **Wordsworth House** on **Main Street** originally belonged to local landowner Sir James Lowther; the poet's father John Wordsworth was Lowther's land agent. William lived here until the tragic death of his mother in 1778, when he was sent to school in Hawkshead. The elegant Georgian building has several rooms furnished in the 18th-century style; on display are a number of articles that belonged to Wordsworth himself. At the back of the house is a walled terraced garden.

Just a few yards away is the **Trout Hotel** (once a private house), which has a connection with a more recent celebrity. Bing Crosby stayed here—in room 18 to be exact—on

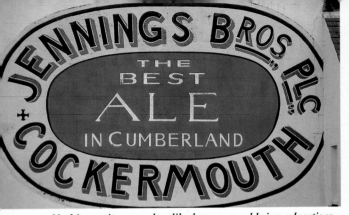

Nothing quite quenches like beer — an old sign advertises the Jennings Brewery in Cockermouth.

one of his trips to England; he used it as a base for a few days of fly-fishing. The hotel is a fascinating amalgamation of architectural styles, with the front section, which houses the cozy bars, being the oldest, dating from around 1670. You can arrange fishing trips through the hotel and lessons during the season.

The **Working Museum of Printing** is also on Main Street; the entrance is through the Printing House shop. This museum documents the history of printing and displays many beautiful and rare manual printing machines dating from the early 1800's. More recent machines saved from destruction include the Linotype printers used to produce newspapers until the advent of digital presses.

Across the river from town is the **Jennings Brewery**, one of the few remaining independent brewers in the area. It supplies many of the pubs in the Lake District — you're sure to see the brewery name on many pub signs. Beer is still brewed by traditional methods here. The brewery runs a regular guided tour, which offers information both about the brewing of beer and about the historic brewery buildings, which stand in the shadow of the ruined Cockermouth Castle. Also on the same site are a **Motor Museum** and the **Cumberland Toy and Model Museum**, which celebrates 100 years of British toy making. Train sets and racing car tracks will bring back childhood memories for many.

Cockermouth has some fascinating little shops. The **Courthouse Antiques and Craft Market**, next to Cocker Bridge, makes an interesting diversion and gives you the opportunity to purchase unusual souvenirs. Antique pieces and collectibles fill every nook and cranny.

Just outside town, on the A5086, is the **Lakeland Sheep and Wool Centre**, where you can meet the woolly creatures of the fells up close. The staff can introduce you to 19 of the over 150 breeds of sheep. They also regularly hold sheep dog and sheep-shearing demonstrations, all in a covered auditorium, which allows you to watch the shepherds at work without having to stand out on the hillsides. You will also find the **Cumwest Exhibition** here, which tells the story of the Western Lakes, the lesser known though no less captivating part of the Lake District.

> Pubs don't have table service. Go to the bar to order your food and drinks.

Thirlmere

The A591—the main route north between Ambleside and Keswick—passes the Thirlmere reservoir, which opened in 1894. There was a great outcry when the city of Manchester to the southeast developed the lake as a reservoir for its swelling population. There were originally two lakes here, as well as a pretty village in the valley. The water company dammed the northern lake, which raised the water level and flooded the village (only after the villagers had been resettled, of course). The main road skirts the eastern side of the lake; the minor route on the west bank, however, is prettier, affording dramatic views of **Helvellyn Peak** in the distance. Helvellyn, 965 m (3116 ft) high, is one of the most popular peaks in the country and forms part of the traditional "Three Peaks Challenge," a 60-km (40-mile) run over the three highest peaks in England—Helvellyn, Scafell Pike, and Skiddaw. You'll always meet fellow ramblers on Helvellyn who'll keep your spirits up if you begin to flag on the ascent.

DAY TRIPS FROM THE LAKE DISTRICT

Gretna Green

About an hour from the Lakes via the M6 is the Scottish village of Gretna Green, which is famous throughout the land for one thing: weddings. In 1753, new legislation in England made it illegal for anyone under the age of 21 to marry without the consent of their parents or legal guardians. This act did not apply in Scotland, however, where 16 remained the age of consent, so many young couples took to eloping to

---

The Post Bus

A curious service found only in rural areas, the post-bus system combines the delivery of mail with a local transport service. For elderly people and others without access to their own transport, the service offers a lifeline for shopping trips and other journeys. Small minibuses of 9–12 seats make regular stops to deliver and pick up mail and passengers along a set route. For a visitor, the post bus is an excellent way to both see the countryside and meet local people.

Scotland, and most stopped to tie the knot in Gretna Green, the nearest town over the border.

The blacksmith's shop in the center of the village became the focus of this activity because it was the blacksmith who often officiated at these ceremonies, striking his anvil with a hammer to signify that the union was official. Getting married "over the anvil" soon became a stock phrase used to refer to the marriage of young couples. Although the laws on marriage changed over the years, the anvil weddings continued, still performed by the amiable blacksmith. Pressure from the church and state eventually forced a ban on anvil weddings, in 1940. Today couples who are nostalgic for the more romantic days of Gretna Green's past still come to **The Old Blacksmith's Shop** to exchange their vows, though they now participate in a legal marriage ceremony. Visitors to the center can view the marriage room, complete with anvil, along with a small museum that has preserved the tales of angry parents who descended on the shop to interrupt weddings in progress. You may be lucky enough to see a wedding yourself. If not, the complex has other diversions, including cafés and a number of shops selling Scottish products from tartan and tweed to whisky.

"I do!"—The village of Gretna Green in Scotland is famous for its weddings.

An old stone roadside distance marker leads travelers from town to town.

To reach Gretna Green, take the M6 north from Penrith. This motorway turns in to A74 and then into the A74(M), Gretna Green is 2 km (1 mile) from junction 2 of the A74(M).

Blackpool

Blackpool has been considered the premier seaside resort in Britain since Victorian times, attracting families from the northern mill towns for fresh air and fun. The town capitalized on its popularity by creating a modern resort full of almost nonstop entertainment. The "golden mile" of the sea-front promenade is packed with people on summer days. Tram lines laid down at the end of the 19th century still carry old trams for those who prefer to ride rather than walk. Candy floss (cotton candy), Blackpool rock (a hard sugar confection), and tacky souvenirs are sold in the many shops that line the promenade: dare yourself to wear a "Kiss me Quick" hat!

The most prominent site in Blackpool is the **Tower**, opened in 1849; some think it served as the inspiration for Tour d'Eiffel in Paris. Take a lift to the top for panoramic views over the town and the sea, or enjoy a genteel tea dance in the ball-room with its ornate chandelier and Wurlitzer organ.

Children can play on the never-ending sandy beach or take a ride on a donkey, a seaside tradition for generations of

English children. For something a little more modern, stop to explore the largest fun fair in the UK, **Blackpool Pleasure Beach**. In the fall Blackpool comes alive with thousands of colored lights that create fanciful pictures and patterns on the sea front. The "illuminations," as they're called, annually draw crowds of thousands, with cars cruising the shore road to watch the show.

To reach Blackpool, take the M6 south from Kendal (junction 36) until you reach the M55 at junction 32, approximately 30 km (20 miles) away. Take the M55, which will lead you to the outskirts of Blackpool, then follow signs for town center.

Hadrian's Wall

When the Roman legions marched into England, they made their way steadily northward until they met with the might of the Scottish Picts. These fierce warriors managed to halt the Roman advance, and a prolonged pitched battle ensued in this borderland. In

> If you want to chat with the locals, comment on the weather, a favorite subject of the British.

122 A.D. the Emperor Hadrian visited Britain and ordered that a defensive wall be built from coast to coast across this territory. Though the Romans occasionally made forays to the north of the wall, this line of fortifications would prove to be the northernmost border of the Roman Empire. It runs some 112 km (70 miles) from Bowness-on-Solway north of Carlisle in the west, to Wallsend, just north of Newcastle-upon-Tyne, in the east.

When the Romans abandoned England at the end of the fourth century A.D., Hadrian's Wall fell into disrepair. Recently designated a World Heritage Site by UNESCO, the wall has been the subject of a great deal of study, and a great number of excavations are now under way all along its path. Many of the remaining intact sections of the wall are now on private land and inaccessible to the public. At Birdoswald Visitors Centre, however, 24 km (15 miles) east of Carlisle, visitors can view the remains of one of the forts and walk along some of the better-preserved sections of the wall. The information center, which serves as a base for archaeologists working at the site, has a number of interesting displays about the history of the wall.

To reach Hadrian's Wall and Birdoswald Visitors Centre, take the M6 north from Penrith. Leave the motorway at junction 43 and take the A69 east. This will take you through the town of Brampton and on to the village of Greenhead. Take a left turn here on the B6318 and after 6 km (4 miles) you will see the sign for Birdoswald.

Settle-to-Carlisle Railway

In the mid-19th century the creation of a network of railway lines revolutionized transport and communications in England. Extending these new lines into remote areas involved vast expense and remarkable feats of engineering. Although many passenger lines have gone out of use as the railroad declined in importance, one line in particular has

The Shepherd's Crook

The shepherd's crook is a vital piece of equipment. It is a walking aid and a tool, the hook at the end being used to pull sheep out of crevices or out of the dipping tank. The crook is also used to signal to the dogs when the wind may be too fierce for a whistle or shouted instruction to be heard. Crooks have traditionally been fashioned from seasoned hazelwood and topped with ram's horn found on the fells.

Perhaps the greatest Roman ruin in the area, Hadrian's Wall was recently designated a World Heritage Site.

been kept in operation, primarily because it travels through some of the most beautiful countryside in Britain. This line runs from Carlisle, the county town of Cumbria, to Settle, a small market town in the neighboring county of North Yorkshire. Passengers can see spectacular views of the Yorkshire Dales National Park and the Eden Valley and then spend some time wandering among the historic stone buildings and the antiques and curio shops of Settle.

On summer weekends, the Railway runs a service with formal lunch—a very refined way to take in the sights. Contact The Settle-Carlisle Information Line, Tel. 066 066 0607 or Cumbria Journey Planner, Tel. (01228) 606000 for more details.

To reach Carlisle, take the M6 north from Penrith, make an exit at junction 43, and take the A69 road left towards Carlisle city center.

WHAT TO DO

OUTDOOR ACTIVITIES

For information about lessons and/or guided group excursions involving some of the activities listed below (climbing, walking, mountain biking, canoeing, and sailing), contact one of the following organizations: Summitreks, 14 Yewdale Road, Coniston, Cumbria LA21 8DU; Tel. (015394) 41212, fax (015394) 41055, or Total Adventure, Holehird Farm, Patterdale Road, Windermere LA23 1NP; Tel. (015394) 47302.

Walking

A paradise for ramblers, the Lake District has a wealth of choices for any level of ability. For the novice or those not in peak condition there are walks or gentle strolls in the valley bottoms and around the lake shores. The paths around Derwent Water and Buttermere are particularly relaxing: They often take in areas of forest, such as at Grizedale, or grassland and park land, as at Mirehouse or Lingholm. Short walks to panoramic viewpoints should be a part of everyone's itinerary. Try Loughrigg and Loughrigg Terrace, easily reached from Grasmere village, for superb views of Windermere and Grasmere lakes. On these walks you'll never be far from a café or pub, so it's always possible to break for lunch or refreshments.

For those who want a slightly more challenging walk, but without a lot of hills to walk up and down, there are a number of routes in the Lake District with little or no gradient. Paths along the windswept bracken fells are for the most part flat and offer spectacular views of surrounding peaks. Examples include routes along Wrynose bottom, around Wast Water, the path along the stream bed at Watendlath, or the course around Blea Tarn in the Langdale Fells; the latter two routes are espe-

Walking is one of the best ways to appreciate the varied landscape and natural beauty of the Lake District.

cially beautiful. These walks are a little more off the beaten track and require advance planning in terms of parking the car and obtaining refreshment, but they're rewarding because of the rich variety of landscapes they cover.

Very fit, experienced walkers enjoy the peak walks, which involve steeper climbs and lead to the very highest points of the Lake District. These require a little more thought, good equipment, and some form of refreshment such as a packed lunch (these can often be prepared by your hotel) as they often take an entire day to complete. The easiest walks in this category are the ones up the popular peaks of Helvellyn or Skiddaw—here you'll find well marked paths and, most times of the year, plenty of company. The most challenging area of all is high above Wasdale. Scafell, Great Gable, Pillar, and Kirk Fell offer challenge and excitement even to the professionals.

Once you assess your own capabilities and make your choice, the options are almost limitless. The tourist information centres throughout the region all have a vast amount of

Calendar of Events

Producing a calendar of events for the Lake District is difficult, since many of the important events such as shows and sports days do not have a set date each year. The following list will give an indication of the time of year certain events take place, but if you want to be in the area for a specific event, please check the date with the Cumbria Tourist Board before making any travel arrangements.

January   *Weekend Book Festival:* Dove Cottage (three days at end of month)

May   *Annual Festival:* Coniston Water (7 days); *Cartmel Steeplechase:* Cartmel (6 days); *Holker Garden Festival:* Holker Hall (3 days); *Medieval Market:* Kendal (1 day); *Victorian Fayre:* Keswick (3 days); All of the above fall toward the end of May.

July   *Rush-Bearing:* Ambleside (4 July); *Agricultural Show:* Penrith (1 day, late in month); *Sports Day:* Ambleside (1 day)

August   *Rush-Bearing:* Grasmere (1 Aug); *Great Summer Show:* Ambleside (early in the month); *Horse Driving Trials:* Lowther (early in the month); *Agricultural Show:* Hawkshead (around 18 Aug); *Sports Day:* Grasmere (around 20 Aug); *Steeplechase:* Cartmel (end of the month)

September   *Westmorland Show:* Kendal (early in the month); *gricultural Society Show:* Loweswater & Brackenthwaite (1 day); *Shepherds Meet:* Borrowdale (one day in middle of the month)

October   *Shepherds Meet and Show:* Wasdale Head (one day); Buttermere (one day in middle of the month); *Power Boat Record Attempts:* Windermere (third week)

November   *Biggest Liar in the World Contest:* Wasdale (18 or 19 November) information on routes for all abilities, as well as maps and charts to help you plan an outing. All footpaths are clearly marked. If you intend to head out onto the fells, though, you should take the appropriate Ordnance Survey map along—they provide the most detailed guides to the terrain.

Visitors who want to do some walking but don't have suitable footwear or equipment should head for one of the larger sporting goods stores in one of the larger towns such as Bowness, Keswick, or Ambleside. Many of these stores rent boots, outerwear, rain gear, and such at daily or weekly rates.

Cycling

Cycling has become extremely popular in the Lakes, even taking into account the fact that some of the roads in the National Park are incredibly steep. For those who would prefer to cycle off-road, there are tracks through the forests at Grizedale and Whinlatter and some well marked cross-country routes. All the major towns have bike-rental shops; ask at hotels or tourist information centers for the location of the nearest "hire center."

Climbing

The area around Wasdale and Scafell offers challenging climbing. If you would like to scale the "highest heights," you'll need expert guidance. For further information contact The British Mountaineering Council, 177–179 Burton Road, West Didsbury, Manchester, M20 2BB; Tel. (0161) 445-4747; fax (0161) 445-4500.

Fishing

Fishing is an extremely popular sport in Britain; with so many lakes to choose from and so much breathtaking countryside all around, the Lake District is an ideal place to try your hand. The region's waters abound in Lakeland char, perch, pike, vendace,

Gone fishing: a local angler relaxes with his rod on the shore of Rydal Water.

and trout. Permits are required, and you will need to buy one separately for each lake. You can get information about rental equipment and permits at the following places: for Ullswater, the Pooley Bridge and Glenridding tourist information centres; for Bassenthwaite Lake, the National Park Information Centre in Keswick; for Coniston Water, Coniston Gifts and Sports in Coniston; and for Derwent Water, the Keswick Anglers Association.

Canoeing and Boating

If you want to get out on the water under your own steam rather than on a lake ferry or steamer, there are a number of ways to do it. At Lake Windermere, Derwent Water, and Ullswater you can rent rowboats (most are big enough for a family of four). At Bowness and Waterhead (Lake Windermere) you will find them lined up next to the ferry piers; at Derwent Water they are found at Lakeside. For Ullswater, travel to Glenridding in the south or Pooley Bridge in the north—in either place you'll find businesses that rent canoes and other water-sports equipment. The local tourist information centres at Windermere, Derwent Water, Ullswater, and Coniston Water have comprehensive information. In addition, the National Trust produces a free "Lake User's Guide" for the following lakes: Ullswater, Coniston, Windermere, Bassenthwaite, and Derwent Water; these booklets have all the information you need to enjoy the water safely. Many lakes or sections of lakes are also wildlife conservation areas; these guides list the regulations that are in effect to protect water birds and other animals. Some of these regulations and restrictions change with the seasons.

Golf

There are golf courses in the following towns: Cockermouth, Kendal, Keswick, Penrith, and Windermere. The golf courses here tend to be much more hilly than most in North America or Australia. The opening hours and rules regarding access vary, so contact the Cumbria Tourist Board in Windermere or one of the local tourist information centers (see page 125) before setting out with your golf bag.

Riding and Pony Trekking

Many equestrian centers throughout the Lake District offer guided rides, which range from easy to challenging. One of the largest centers is near Coniston, and there are several around Ullswater. Public bridle paths throughout the Lake District lead through particularly beautiful and tranquil countryside. Contact the Cumbria Tourist Board or local tourist information centers for full details (see page 125).

For information about lessons and/or group excursions, try Armathwaite Hall, Equestrian Centre, Coalbeck Farm,

Bassenthwaite, Keswick; Tel. (017687) 76949 (open year-round), or Park Foot Trekking Centre, Pooley Bridge, Ullswater; Tel. (017684) 86696 (open March–October).

Photography

With its variety of landscapes and ever-changing light, the Lake District offers never-ending opportunities for outdoor photographers. Standard print film is available in many shops in the major towns, but serious shutterbugs will want to seek out one of the following photography stores for a full range of specialist film and equipment: Abbey Photographic, 25, Stramongate, Kendal LA9 4BH; Tel. (01539) 720-085, or The Photo Shop, North Road, Ambleside, Cumbria LA22 9 DT; Tel. (015394) 34375.

LAKELAND SOCIAL EVENTS

Agricultural shows

Every farming community in the Lake District has one day in the year when it comes together to celebrate its way of life and compete at various events. These are a traditional part of country life—they're not staged as tourist attractions, but visitors are always welcome. Local farmers bring their livestock and engage in serious rivalry for the champion rosettes. The prizes are often mere trinkets—the real payoff is when the animal comes to market, since a prize ram, for example, can make a lot of money at market later in the year. Family pride mixes with economics at these events. Farming can be a lonely life, and even in modern times it is rare for the families to take time off from the hard work and socialize. These agricultural shows offer families the opportunity to get together and have fun, and they offer visitors a rare chance to chat with the local farming community.

Each summer the sheepdog trials offer a friendly competition for farmers and their dogs.

Sheepdog trials

The way sheepdogs do their job is a source of fascination for visitors and of pride to the farmers who breed and train them. Each summer local farmers and their dogs get together for a friendly competition; the dog and farmer maneuver sheep around a set course. Both speed and accuracy are assessed to decide the winner. Remember as you watch these skillful operators that they cheerfully perform the same tasks in snowdrifts and the thickest fog and cloud in the depths of winter.

Lakeland Sports Days

The men of the Lakes, hard working and abstemious, have always found ways to enjoy themselves, and this more often than not involved means physical competition. A number of sporting contests have become part of Lakeland tradition. Before the advent of cars it was common to see hundreds of people walking towards the show-grounds, and often the best sportsmen from neighboring valleys came over the fells to compete.

The sports days are still taken as seriously by competitors today as they were one hundred years ago. Winners still become local celebrities and their reputation reaches to the very corners of the Lakes.

One of the sports that developed in the Lake District is a unique form of wrestling. Two men stand face to face with their arms wrapped around each other's body, hands clasped tightly together behind the other's back. The men then try to unbalance their opponent. The first man to hit the ground with a part of the body other than the feet loses the contest.

Fell running also tests the mettle. Competitors simply run up and down the side of a fell, taking obstacles like bogs, streams, and rocks in their stride. The fastest man wins.

Hound trailing, also once a part of daily life, remains a popular sport. This is how it works in today's competitions: an aniseed-scented trail is laid on the morning of the race, and the dogs are sent off across the fells to follow it, disappearing out

Members of the Morris Dancers don their distinctive red vests and flowered hats for a special performance.

of sight through the bracken. Although the prize money is negligible, you would not think so when the dogs reappear and the enthusiastic owners call, whistle, and wave them home.

Hunting for live prey is still an important part of country life, but less popular than in John Peel's day (see page 64). Lake District hunters follow the pack on foot rather than using horses because the incline of the fells is too difficult for horses.

Summer Festivals

The towns, not to be outdone by the agricultural shows, also hold annual festivals such as the popular Victorian Festival at Keswick or the Medieval Festival in Kendal; both are in late May and both feature crafts, food stalls, and artists and entertainers in period costumes. Many of the country houses also hold special events, such as antiques or crafts fairs or "fun days" with fair rides, throughout the summer months. Check with the tourist information centers for details about these and similar events at Dalemain, Holker Hall, and Muncaster Castle.

Rush Bearing

Rushes taken from the lakes were traditionally used to carpet church floors in the Lake District, and once a year, to refresh this floor covering, children from the village would ceremonially carry a new batch of rushes into the church. This tradition has survived, though today in many places the children bear flowers or fruit rather than rushes. Two good places to witness the rush-bearing ceremony are St. Mary's Parish Church in Ambleside (4 July) and Grasmere Parish Church in Grasmere (1 August).

SHOPPING

Natural raw materials found in the area have been used for centuries to make beautiful decorative objects. Slate, horn, wool, and wood were always used to make tools and implements, but these materials are now also being used in the production of interesting souvenirs. Favorite items that will help preserve your memories of the rugged Lakeland countryside are clothing or blankets made from the local Herdwick wool, coasters of polished slate, or walking sticks with ram's-horn handles.

Crafts such as ceramics and pottery-making, wood-turning, and glass-blowing are also popular. Many individual crafts-people work in the Lake District, and as you wander you'll find signs leading you to their studios in converted barns and other outbuildings. The prices are not necessarily low, but the quality of these hand-crafted objects is high. Although every town has shops that sell these items, a good place to start would be the Made in Cumbria shop situated in the Tourist Information Centre in Windermere; they stock a wide range of locally produced handicrafts.

Visual artists find the natural beauty of the Lake District in-spiring, and their paintings or photographs make fitting sou-venirs. You'll find galleries in all the major towns and in some of the smaller villages. If you find yourself in the village of Boot, go to the Fold End Gallery; Tel. (019467) 23316 (open Easter–Christmas daily 10:30–5:30, longer in summer). Heaton Cooper and his son are among the most prestigious landscape painters of the century; visit their studio opposite the village green in Grasmere (open daily); Tel. (015394) 35280. Throughout the region you'll come across limited-edition prints signed by the artist; these make good mementos. Just pick your favorite view and it will bring you years of pleasure.

Since the Lake District is so popular for outdoor activities, it's a good place to shop for outdoor clothing and equipment. All the major towns have several shops with jackets, hats, boots, rain gear, etc. There are good bargains to be found at the end of each season, particularly just after Christmas, when the shops of towns like Ambleside have seasonal sales.

Blackpool Tower looms beyond the festive streets of Blackpool in Lancashire.

If it's foodstuffs you're after, there are some unusual offerings in the Lakes. Cumberland sausage is the local specialty. Award winner Richard Woodall, who has a royal warrant to supply sausages to Queen Elizabeth II, is one of the manufacturers to look for. Woodall's also prepares delicious hams from home-reared animals. The family shop is at Waberthwaite just south of Ravensglass, but you will find his produce in food stores across the Lakes.

Kendal Mint Cake is packaged in fancy gift boxes but you don't need to be going on an expedition to enjoy it. Sara

Curious marine buffs soak in the sights at Lakeside's Aquarium of the Lakes.

Nelson's Gingerbread, made and sold at their shop in Grasmere, can be bought in pretty tins to take home.

Markets are a good way to get a feel for everyday life. In the Lake District the gentleman farmer and his wife come into town to shop on market day. Particularly busy, colorful markets include those in Kendal (Monday, Wednesday, Saturday), Keswick (Saturday), and Penrith (Tuesday, Saturday).

The cattle and sheep markets are not tourist attractions as such. However, for those who want to get a behind-the-scenes view of real Lakeland life, these events are hard to beat. Just be discreet, and don't wear your best shoes. Try Cockermouth (Monday and Wednesday) or Penrith (Tuesday).

THE LAKE DISTRICT FOR CHILDREN

There are so many things for children to do in the great outdoors of the Lake District. They can paddle in the streams, go bird-watching, or cycle on the trails in Grizedale or Whinlatter forests. Afternoon hikes and picnics are also pleasant diversions. Trying their hand at fishing or rowing a boat on a lake can be a challenge. More organized activities include joining a horseback-riding or canoeing expedition. Particularly good family outings—if the weather is fine—are trips to see the animals at Trotters and Friends in Bassenthwaite or at the Owl Sanctuary at Muncaster Castle, or taking steam-railway rides at Lakeside or on La'al Ratty at Eskdale. And a trip on a lake ferry can be run in any sort of weather.

Rainy days are the most challenging for parents, but there are still plenty of attractions to fill the time. Try the Aquarium of the Lakes at Lakeside, the Pencil Museum at Keswick, or the World of Beatrix Potter Exhibition at Bowness.

NIGHTLIFE

The Lake District is not the place to come if you want lots of action into the early morning hours. Don't expect to be swinging much after midnight, even in towns.

Theater

There is a lively theater scene in the Lake District during the summer, but many performances can be fully booked months ahead. The tourist information offices will have details of the programs. You can also obtain information directly from the following venues: The Theatre in the Forest at Grizedale; Tel. (01229) 860291, Brewery Arts Centre, 122a Highgate, Kendal; Tel. (01539) 725133, Century Theatre in Keswick; Tel. (017687) 74411, The Old Laundry Theatre, Crag Brow, Bowness-on-Windermere; Tel. (01539) 88444.

Cinema

There are a number of cinemas in the Lake District that show the latest British releases and sometimes schedule retrospectives. Zeffirelli's on Compston Road in Ambleside is a cinema

A bartender pulls a pint at one of the many local pubs of the Lake District.

and restaurant complex where you can make a night of it with a movie and a meal.

Pubs

Every village and town has at least one Public House, or pub, where alcoholic drinks are served to adults (the drinking age is 18). Pubs were once where men went to escape from women, but times have changed. Many pubs now serve meals and have entertainment; chalkboards outside the pub will let you know when they're having live music or other events. Some pubs have pool tables and darts or TV sets, which are usually tuned to sports events, more likely than not a football (soccer) game. Family rooms have been introduced in many spots, making it easier for younger children to enjoy meals with their parents (and vice versa). Many outside beer gardens—very popular when the weather is fine—also now have children-friendly areas. Each pub has its own unique atmosphere, created by the landlord and the local clientele. If you stay in the Lake District for more than a few days you're sure to find a favorite.

Last call at pubs is at 11 sharp, to ensure that guests don't linger much beyond 11:15. Local hotels with drink licenses can serve guests later than 11, often until the guests themselves decide to call it a night.

EATING OUT

Traditional Lakeland Foods

For centuries the people of the Lakeland have subsisted on their own local produce: mutton from the hillsides; wild birds, such as pheasant, which are still seen in great numbers in Grizedale Forest; ducks from the surface of the lakes and fresh fish from the water. Pride of place among the many varieties of fish found here has always belonged to the native Lakeland char. A relative of the salmon and trout, this fish evolved here over centuries of isolation and is found only in the Lake District.

Game meats such as hare and venison were also plentiful, but for many years the latter was only available to the lord of the manor. Peasants could only get venison by poaching, a crime punishable by death or banishment. In peasant homes, meat was cooked with vegetables in pies and pastries to make a little go a long way. Preserving meats and vegetables to make them last through the long winters was a highly valued skill. Sausages and salted hams would keep for many weeks in a cool larder; fruits and vegetables were preserved in pickles, chutneys, and jams. Today these traditional dishes form the basis of many menus in Lake District restaurants.

Now, that's a sausage! A local butcher displays a regional specialty.

In the 16th and 17th centuries trade with the English colonies in the West Indies grew, and new ingredients filtered into Lakeland cooking. The ports of the west coast of Cumbria were extremely important at that time, and many of the imported foodstuffs, such as rum and spices, became easily available. Rum butter, traditionally used as an accompaniment to Christmas pudding, became a Lakeland specialty, and more ordinary local foods, such as the humble sausage, started to become a good deal spicier.

Fine Dining

In the Victorian and Edwardian eras many wealthy visitors came to spend time in the Lake District, and local innkeepers and restaurant owners worked hard to ensure that the quality of food and service they provided matched their visitors' expectations. Later, as the number of English Country House Hotels began to grow, the practice of serving fine food with silver service in the English manner, continued. These traditions carry on to the present day.

There have always been a large number of fine restaurants in the Lake District, and you will have no difficulty finding "award-winning" food served in elegant restaurants or dining rooms. Four- or five-course meals complete with aperitifs, fine wines, and digestifs with coffee are what many English travelers have come to expect in these genteel establishments. Prepare to put on weight during your stay.

If you prefer something simpler than a grand meal in a country house, you'll have no trouble choosing from among the many smaller and less-formal places to eat in the Lakelands. You'll find bistros in all the main towns, along with a number of Italian restaurants that serve the usual range of pasta dishes and good-value house wines. Chinese and Indian restaurants are also beginning to establish themselves.

Pub Food

Eating in Public Houses is a good option, especially if you are on a budget, although many or them now also have more formal restaurant settings and fine menus. Traditionally, pub food meant good, basic home cooking—pies with vegetables, stews, or snacks such as the traditional British sandwich. These are still to be found on every menu, but pub food is becoming a little more imaginative. Thai and Indian dishes are growing in popularity, as are "jacket potatoes" (large potatoes cooked in their skins and topped with various sauces). Another favorite, especially in the summer, is the so-called "ploughman's lunch"—chunks of local cheese or ham with pickles, chutney, and crusty bread. You can often eat well in a pub for under £10 per head, which is extremely good value.

Fast Food

For those who crave fast food, the Lake District may prove disappointing. The international chains are only just beginning to make inroads into the area. It is possible to get a burger in Kendal if you really crave one. Other then that, it is back to that traditional English fast-food favorite, fish and chips—fried fish in batter and chips (French fries), which are normally wrapped in paper and eaten outside.

Puddings

Traditional English puddings are still very popular; you will find a range of them on restaurant menus. Hot sweets made of flour, sugar, and butter (or suet from the loins and kidneys of sheep) and filled with currants, apples, plums, or jam, they are either boiled, steamed, or baked in the oven. They are always served with a sweet custard sauce. Try bread-and-butter pudding: layers of bread with dried fruit, sugar, milk, and just a little rum.

A typical English breakfast is a great way to start a day of walking and sightseeing in the Lake District.

Sandwiches

Invented by the Earl of Sandwich so that he could stay at the gambling tables and eat at the same time, this early form of TV dinner is on the menu at every café and pub. The fillings range from the mundane—roast beef or roast ham—to the more exotic—chicken in curry mayonnaise—and can be made with almost any form of bread known, from plain white teacakes to French baguettes and Italian ciabattas.

English Breakfast

Although few people prepare a full English breakfast at home anymore (except perhaps on Sunday), it is a standard part of a Lakeland holiday. All hotels, inns, B&B's, and guest houses have it on the menu, and it's almost always included in the price of your room. A traditional cooked breakfast consists of eggs (poached or fried), bacon, sausage, black pudding (blood sausage), and a choice of mushrooms or beans. All of this is preceded by cereal and fruit juice and accompanied by toast, jam, and tea or coffee. As you might imagine, this can fortify you quite well for the day. If you're traveling on a budget, eating a full English breakfast is one way of making your money go farther—you may not even need lunch!

Afternoon Tea

Another English tradition in genteel circles is the practice of taking Afternoon Tea. This was generally something that ladies did while the men were out at the office or the gentleman's club. Today it's a wonderful way to spend an afternoon, but don't expect to be able to manage dinner later in the day. The food consists of small sandwiches—cucumber, usually—and a selection of cakes and scones with butter and jam. Properly brewed tea accompanies the food, of course.

The taking of Afternoon Tea is as much about ceremony as it is about food. It is an occasion. The tea must be brewed in a china or silver teapot and served in china cups with saucers and matching tea plates; the cakes must be served on an elegant cake stand. The patron should then leave you to enjoy the ritual at your leisure, so it's well worth finding somewhere elegant to do it.

Beverages

The UK is infamous worldwide for two drinks—tea and warm beer—though in reality there are many more options for liquid refreshment.

Tea is still the national drink in the UK and it can be found everywhere. There are many proprietary brands of tea—blends of mixed leaves created to meet the producer's specifications. Often these are produced for selling all across the country, but tea may also be blended to suit local water conditions or to suit certain times of day—breakfast tea, for example, is a light refreshing tea, ideal to wake up with.

You can also find tea produced from the leaf of one specific variety of plant or from one particular geographical area, such as Darjeeling, from India. There are also a number of teas blended to produce a particular flavor, such as Earl Gray, flavored with bergamot (fragrant oil from the rind of a small citrus fruit). Fruit teas are also available. If tea isn't your "cup of tea," don't worry; you'll find coffee everywhere, too.

Yes, English beer is traditionally served at room temperature. Today's English breweries produce a range of brews, from light "pale ale" through "bitter" to "stout," which is the heaviest in constitution. If you want to try something new, ask the pub landlord for advice. Some pubs, such as the Cavendish at Cartmel, sell "real ales," which are brewed using traditional methods (usually at small, independent breweries). The name of the brewer will be found on a sign outside the pub. Jennings Brewery based in Cockermouth is a name you will often. If you see the phrase "Free House" on a pub sign it means that this public house has no affiliation with any particular brewery. You will also be able to find many types of lager beer in addition to the traditional ales. Beer from the barrel is served in "pint" or "half" measures. A range of bottled Continental and American beers have become available in recent years, so look out for them on the chilled shelf behind the bar.

The UK produces very little of its own wine, but this is a very popular drink, reflected in the range of wines available in shops and restaurants. You will be able to find wine from all over the world. The wine lists of most restaurants will have a selection of French, Italian, and Spanish wines along with the extremely popular "new world" wines from the US, Australia, New Zealand, South Africa, and Chile.

INDEX

HANDY TRAVEL TIPS

An A–Z Summary of Practical Information

A

ACCOMMODATIONS (See also CAMPING, YOUTH HOSTELS, and the list of Recommended Hotels starting on page 129)

The Lake District has a full range of accommodations but very few big hotels; a hotel with 30 bedrooms is considered large in this region. For this reason you can almost always be assured of getting a personal touch wherever you decide to stay. The owners are often very involved in the running of their establishments, and they will make every effort to ensure that you are happy with your stay.

The British Tourist Authority uses a quality rating system for all types of accommodations throughout the country. In their directories, "crown"symbols are used to designate hotels, guest houses, and B&B's, and "key" symbols are used for self-catering accommodations. All establishments are graded on a scale of 1 to 5 crowns or keys; the more facilities and amenities a given lodging has to offer, the higher the number of crowns or keys. All the establishments listed in the BTA directories offer at a bare minimum cooked or Continental breakfast, heating and hot water at no extra cost, clean towels and soap, and clean bedding in sound condition. Next to the crowns or keys you'll find one of the following evaluations: "approved," "commended," "highly commended," or "deluxe." These ratings have to do with the quality of the decor, furnishings, amenities, and hospitality. Take both of these rating systems into consideration when you're trying to choose a place to stay. For example, a three-crown "highly commended" hotel may offer a more satisfying stay over all than a four-crown "approved" hotel.

Over all, there are four categories of accommodations in Britain. **B&B's** offer just that: a bed for the night and an English or Continental breakfast. Many are very small establishments or private homes. There are few or no extra facilities available, and you may be required to share toilet and bath with other guests. **Guest houses** are generally larger establishments with more rooms than B&B's; they may also offer a set evening meal. **Hotels** generally have rooms with private facilities and more amenities. Many hotels are converted houses and, even in up-market establishments, rooms can vary in size; be specific about your needs when you make reservations to make sure you get a room that meets them. **Inns** are public houses (pubs) that also have rooms to rent. In the Lake District these were often coach houses on traditional routes.

Prices for hotel rooms in Britain are generally quoted per person, rather than per room, and a supplement is usually added for a single traveler. It's worth noting that even some of the best upscale hotels also offer so-called "B&B" rates.

The Cumbria Tourist Board offices throughout the Lake District can provide detailed lists of B&B's, guest houses, hotels, and inns. They can also arrange for you to stay on a working farm. Ask for the booklet *Farmhouse Vacations,* published by the British Tourist Authority. Contact any of their regional offices or the main office of the Cumbria Tourist Board in Windermere (see TOURIST INFORMATION OFFICES).

The Cumbria Tourist Board also operates a booking hotline, which you can use to make reservations before or during your trip; Tel. (0808) 100 8848. Local tourist information offices will be able to book accommodations for you while you're traveling, but it's not advisable to arrive without reservations during the summer; from late June until early September it may be difficult to find the right kind of accommodations on the spot. If you need to book accommodations after you arrive in the United Kingdom but before you reach the Lake District, you can do this at the BTA information kiosks at Heathrow and Manchester airports. Most tourists approach the Lake District from the south, arriving first at Windermere; the tourist office there, just next door to the train station, is a good place to get information about accommodations throughout the region (see TOURIST INFORMATION OFFICES).

AIRPORTS (See also GETTING THERE)

International flights to London arrive at either Heathrow Airport, Britain's main air transport hub, or Gatwick Airport. The airport closest to the Lake District is Manchester International, the main airport in northern England. (It's about a 1½ hour drive from the airport to the central lakes.) American, British Airways, Delta, Continental, Air Canada, and Aer Lingus all have direct flights from the US; British Airways and British Midland have numerous daily connections from Heathrow and Gatwick. British Airways also operates between Manchester and Canada, Australia, New Zealand, South Africa, and Ireland. Excellent connections are available between Manchester and several hubs in Europe, including Amsterdam, Paris, and Frankfurt. Quantas and Air New Zealand fly to London Heathrow.

From Heathrow there are tube and rail links into central London for connections to train and bus routes to the rest of the country. The Gatwick Express rail link takes passengers from Gatwick to central London. Manchester Airport operates Manchester Airport Railway Station, which provides fast and efficient service to many parts of the country (see GETTING THERE).

B

BICYCLE RENTAL

Cycle tracks and bridle ways abound in the Lake District, and there are many places to rent bicycles, including mountain bikes, which are ideal for much of the terrain. The local tourist information offices have details of what's available in their immediate area. Millennium Cycles has rental centers at Windermere, Bowness, and Kendal, as well as in Grizedale. The average cost is £8 per day. A number of companies also organize bike tours; on some of these itineraries your luggage is transported by van so that it's waiting for you at your lodging at the end of the day. These tours start at about £25 per day. Contact the Cumbria Tourist Board in Windermere for details; Tel. (015394) 444 444.

BUDGETING for YOUR TRIP

The UK is an expensive destination to visit. Below are some guidelines on prices that should help you prepare for your trip.

Accommodations. For room and breakfast in a moderately priced hotel, allow £50 per person. Spending a little more on a D, B&B (dinner, bed, and breakfast) plan at a hotel will provide you with a good three- or four-course evening meal at a cheaper price than you would find at a restaurant; allow around £15–£18 per person for this option. Staying in a small B&B will run around £25 per person (you'll probably pay more if you want a private bath and toilet). Self-catering cottages for two people will range from £150–£350 per week, depending on the season; for family-size accommodations, allow £300–£1000.

Meals. For lunch in a decent, moderately priced place allow £15 per person plus drinks; for dinner, £25 per person plus drinks. Prices are lower in pubs and higher in first-class restaurants. Many restaurants serve lunch specials or "early-bird" specials in the evenings (usually before 6:45pm); look out for these as they will help you to save money.

Car rental. Allow around £200 per week for a medium sized car (see also CAR RENTAL).

Public transportation

Full-day tour by bus (small 12–15-seater) is £20–£25.

Round-trip train fare from London to Windermere ranges from £56 (after 9:30am and not between 3:30pm and 6:30pm Mon–Thur, Sat, and Sun) to £132 (before 9:30am and between 3:30pm and 6:30pm weekdays and all day Friday).

One-way train fare from Manchester to Windermere is £26.60 on Fri, £25.30 every other day of the week.

A Day Rover ticket on Stagecoach Cumberland (local bus services) is £5.50.

A 4-Day Rover ticket is £13.50.

Freedom of the Lakes ticket: (combining lake cruisers and buses) £9.50 for adults, £5.00 children (see PUBLIC TRANSPORTATION).

C

CAMPING

There are a number of camping sites throughout the Lake District. There are also a small number of "camping barns" that offer basic facilities available for rent; you need to supply your own bedding and cooking equipment, and some people even set up tents inside the barns for extra comfort. The Cumbria Tourist Board rates the camping sites from one to five, with five being the highest quality; contact them for more details (see TOURIST INFORMATION OFFICES).

CAR RENTAL

Having a car allows you the freedom to travel where you want exactly when you want, especially in the more remote areas of the National Park. Unfortunately none of the major car-rental companies have offices in the Lake District, so you will have to make arrangements to pick up a car in a nearby major city such as York, Leeds, or Carlisle before continuing on into the Lakes. All the major car-rental companies—Hertz, Avis, and Europcar—have desks at the London and Manchester airports, and it is possible to pick up a car from the airport immediately upon your arrival in the UK.

Some of the larger companies offer more competitive rates if you reserve the car from home. It pays, therefore, to sketch out your itinerary before departing for the UK so that you can make a reservation and plan pick-up and drop-off points before you depart. All companies offer special rates at certain times of the year, so ask when you call. Smaller local companies, such as Thrifty, offer cheaper rates.

Car rental in the UK is expensive, but the vehicles are new and kept in excellent condition. A small car will cost around £200 per week, medium-size cars around £270. All companies charge approximately £50 more per week for a car with automatic transmission. Insurance covers collision damage and theft, but personal accident insurance runs an extra £3 or £4 per day. Many companies have a minimum age, usually between 23 and 25. Credit cards are preferred, and you will need to show your drivers license when you pick up the car.

CLIMATE

Britain has a temperate climate influenced by its proximity to the Atlantic Ocean—the summers and warm and wet and the winters are cold and wet. Even in summer, though, there can be cold spells, and on higher ground such as the fells and peaks of the Lake District, the weather can change quickly. The following chart shows the average daytime temperatures for each month, along with the average amount of rainfall and average hours of sunshine per month.

	J	F	M	A	M	J	J	A	S	O	N	D
Temperature °F	38	42	45	50	58	62	65	63	60	52	44	42
Temperature °C	4	5	7	10	14	17	19	18	15	11	7	6
Rainfall in inches	2	1.75	1.75	1.75	1.9	1.8	2.2	2.2	2	2.1	2.3	1.9
Hours of sunshine	1	2	4	5	6	7	6	6	5	3	2	1

The Lake District has a telephone weather service, updated daily; Tel. (017687) 75757. Many hotels also post the weather forecast for the day in the foyer or reception area.

CLOTHING

Even in the summer the weather in the Lake District can be change-able and the high fells attract clouds, so it's best to pack clothing that you can layer easily; this way you can add or take off items depend-ing on how warm or cool you feel. In winter you'll need heavy jack-ets and sweaters, but in summer, shorts and lightweight top layers will do. Make sure that you carry a windproof layer or a fleece sweater or vest to be prepared for sudden drops in temperature. Never attempt a fell walk without adequate clothing. If you intend to do any serious or difficult walking or hiking, it's essential you take along proper weatherproof clothing. Sensible comfortable shoes are essential no matter where you are in the Lakelands, and for fell walk-ing or hiking you will need sturdy walking boots. Many of the sport-ing goods stores in the major towns rent clothing, footwear, and equipment by the day or week, and at the very least these stores are a good source of advice when you're preparing for an outing.

Casual clothing is standard throughout the Lakes. Slacks, warm jackets, and comfortable shoes are appropriate for most situations. Casual attire is the rule in pubs and most restaurants. Some of the smarter restaurants and hotels, however, have a more formal dress code, which often means jacket and tie for men.

COMPLAINTS

Complaints should first be made to the establishment or individual concerned. If this does not resolve the issue, there are various bodies in Britain that deal with different forms of complaint. Contact the nearest office of the British Tourist Authority for a referral to the appropriate authorities (see TOURIST INFORMATION OFFICES).

CRIME and SAFETY

The United Kingdom is relatively free from major crime and the Lake District has even fewer major crimes than the larger towns and cities. It is safe to walk in the downtown areas of the cities at night. As it is no matter where you're traveling, however, common sense should always prevail. Leaving valuables in full view when you leave the car is an open invitation to thieves. Lock all valuables in the trunk and check items you won't need for the day in the hotel safe or with the front desk.

Lake District

As far as safety on the fells is concerned, if you intend to walk on any high ground be sure to inform someone of your intended route and timing. Many hotels encourage their guests to lodge a "walk plan" with the front desk before they set out so that the hotel staff can inform the mountain rescue squad or other emergency services about your route if there is a problem. Remember to also let hotel staff and others know when you've returned from your excursion.

CUSTOMS and ENTRY REQUIREMENTS

Citizens of the US, Canada, Ireland, Australia, and New Zealand, need only a valid passport to enter the United Kingdom for a holiday. Citizens of South Africa are required to show a valid passport and a return ticket. All passports must be valid for six months beyond the intended length of stay in the UK.

Visitors arriving from non-EU countries are allowed to bring into the UK: 200 cigarettes or 50 cigars or 250 grams of tobacco; 1 liter of alcohol over 22 proof or 2 liters of alcohol of less than 22 proof or 2 liters of fortified or sparkling wine; 2 liters of wine; 50 grams of perfume or 250 ml of toilet water; and other goods to the value of £136.

Upon arrival you will have to fill in an entry card stating the address where you will be staying. The immigration officer will stamp your passport, allowing you to stay in Britain for a specific length of time. If your plans are uncertain ask for several months so you don't have to apply for an extension later. Provided you look respectable and have sufficient funds to cover your stay there should not be a problem.

In British ports and airports, passengers with goods to declare follow the red channel; those with nothing to declare follow the green.

Currency restrictions. There is no limit on how much foreign currency you may import into Britain, and the export of pounds is not restricted. Check to see whether your own country has any regulations on the import and export of currency.

DRIVING

If you are bringing in your own car or one from Europe you will need the registration papers and insurance coverage. The usual formula is the Green Card, an extension to the normal insurance, validating it for other countries.

Road conditions. Remember to drive on the left. Pay special attention at corners (crossings) and traffic circles (roundabouts). Traffic that is already in the circle has the right of way over cars waiting to enter the circle, and the rule is to give way to the right.

There are three main types of roads: motorways (expressways), A roads (trunk roads that link all the major towns), and B roads (rural roads). Driving conditions in the UK are generally very good, and all A roads are of good quality. In the Lake District and other similar rural areas, however, the B roads and a few unclassified roads are narrow and winding and they are often not clearly divided into two lanes. Many Lakeland routes also have some fairly steep climbs and descents, and it's not unusual to find sheep or slow-moving farm machinery blocking your way. Over all, you'll need to exercise caution and patience, as well as your sense of humor.

Some single-lane roads in the Lake District are so narrow that it's impossible to pass the car in front of you. On such roads you'll find periodic passing places—wider spots where it's possible to overtake the car ahead of you or get out of the way of approaching traffic; these may or may not be signposted. If a passing place appears on the left of the road, move into it to let faster-moving cars behind you pass. If the passing place is on the right, stop in the roadway to let an approaching vehicle move into the passing place. Where possible, always stop for a vehicle coming up a hill. If an approaching driver is flashing his lights on such a narrow road, it usually means "please proceed," though do note that this signal is not listed in the official *Highway Code* guide. It can be slightly confusing at first; it's best to approach every encounter on these narrow roads with caution.

Rules and regulations. Drivers and front-seat passengers must use seat belts; rear-seat passengers must also use seat belts if available. Motorcycle riders must wear a crash helmet and a driver's license is required for all types of motorcycle. Sixteen is the lower age limit for mopeds, seventeen for motorcycles and scooters.

In built-up urban areas the speed limit is 48 or 64 km/h (30 or 40 mph); on expressways and two-lane highways 112 km/h (70 mph);

and on most other roads 80 or 96 km/h (50 or 60 mph). The speed limit is posted on round signs at the side of the road.

Fuel costs. Gasoline is expensive in the UK—approximately 65p per liter. Most garages have self-service pumps, all of which give measurements in liters. You will find stations in all major towns. The normal hours of operation for fuel are 9am–5:30pm, but this can vary enormously. Hours are extended in the summer months. It's always best to check fuel levels before embarking on a journey over the passes or into the most rural areas around the Lakes.

Fluid measures

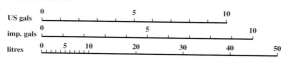

Distance

Parking. You can park on the roadside if there are no posted restrictions. Parking is prohibited by entrances to farms and fields or in passing places. Car parks throughout the Lakes operate on a "Pay and Display" system—you purchase a ticket from a machine (normally situated right in the car park) and display the ticket on your dashboard.

If you need help. Most rental cars come with coverage from a reputable recovery or breakdown service. The Automobile Association (AA), the Royal Automobile Club (RAC), and Green Flag are the most well-known.

AA: Norfolk House, Priestley Road, Basingstoke, Hampshire RG24 9NY; Tel. (0345) 500600, breakdowns Tel. (0800) 887766.

RAC: RAC House, 1 Forest Road, Feltham. TW13 7RR. Travel Information; Tel. (0891) 347-333, breakdowns Tel. (0800) 828282.

Green Flag: Green Flag House, Cote Lane, Pudsey, West Yorkshire, LS28 5GF. Tel. (0800) 000 111, breakdowns Tel. (0800) 400 600.

Road signs. Britain has adopted the same basic system of pictographs in use throughout Europe. The *Highway Code* is the official booklet of road usage and signs, available at most bookshops. The following written signs may not be instantly comprehensible:

British	*American*
Carriageway	Roadway
Clearway	No parking by highway
Diversion	Detour
Dual carriageway	Divided highway
Give way	Yield
Level crossing	Railroad crossing
Motorway	Expressway
No overtaking	No passing
Roadworks	Men working
Roundabout	Traffic circle

E

ELECTRIC CURRENT

The standard current in England is 240 volt, 50 cycle AC. All visitors (except South Africans) will need an adapter (with square 3-pin plugs) for any appliance brought from home, as well as a converter unless the appliance is equipped with one. Adapters are available at airport shops. Most hotels have special sockets for shavers and hairdryers that operate on 240 or 110 volts.

EMBASSIES, CONSULATES, HIGH COMMISSIONS

All of the following are in London and open to the public Monday–Friday (the visa section is often open for only part of the day):

Australia	Australia House, The Strand, WC2B 4LA; Tel. (0171) 379-4334
Canada	MacDonald House, 1 Grosvenor Square, W1X 0AB; Tel. (0171) 258-6600
Ireland	Irish Embassy, 17 Grosvenor Place, SW1X 7HR; Tel. (0171) 235-2171

Lake District

New Zealand	New Zealand House, 80 Haymarket, SW1Y 4TQ; Tel. (0171) 930-8422
South Africa	South Africa House, Trafalgar Square, WC2N 5DP; Tel. (0710) 930-4488
US	24 Grosvenor Square, W1A 1AE; Tel. (0710) 499-9000

EMERGENCIES

For police, the fire brigade, or an ambulance dial 999 from any telephone (no money or card required) and tell the operator which service you require. In the Lake District it's also very helpful if you have as many details as possible about your location when you call.

G

GETTING THERE (see also AIRPORTS)

By Air

Most international flights to the UK arrive at either Heathrow or Gatwick. The international airport nearest to the Lake District is at Manchester, which is also served by connecting flights from Heathrow and Gatwick. From North America there are direct flights to London from Atlanta, Boston, Chicago, Dallas/Fort Worth, Los Angeles, Montreal, New York, San Francisco, Toronto, and a number of smaller hubs; now there is also direct service from many of these same cities to Manchester. From Australia and New Zealand there are several weekly flights to London from Sydney, Melbourne, Perth, and Auckland. Most flights to the UK from South Africa land in London.

Tube (subway) and rail links transport passengers from London's Heathrow to central London for connections to mainline rail stations and bus services. London Gatwick airport operates the Gatwick Express rail link into central London. There are also taxi services from the airport terminals. Manchester Airport operates the Manchester Airport Railway Station for easy and convenient direct services and connections to many parts of the country.

By Train

Virgin trains run from London's Paddington Station and Manchester's International Airport Railway Station to Kendal in the

Lake District and the nearby cities of Penrith and Carlisle. The travel time is approximately three hours. Call the Virgin TrainLine for schedules and fare information; Tel. (0345) 222-333.

By Bus

National Express Coaches operate services to Kendal and onward into the Lake District from most cities in Britain. Travel time from London's Victoria Station is approximately 6½ hours. For information and reservations, call (0990) 808-080.

By Road

All major car rental companies have offices at the London airports and at Manchester airport (see CAR RENTAL). The M6 motorway skirts the Lake District, offering easy access to the gateway towns of Kendal and Penrith and then on into the National Park. From Manchester Airport the driving time is approximately 1½ hours on the M56 and M6; from London it's approximately five hours via the M40, M42, and M6.

GUIDES and TOURS

Cumbria's official "Blue Badge" guides provide assistance to individuals or to groups of walkers, as well as to visitors traveling by car or by bus. They are also prepared to provide tours and information in several languages. You can arrange for a guide by contacting one of the tourist information centers or the Blue Badge central booking office at Mickle Bower, Temple Sowerby, Penrith CA10 1RZ; Tel. (017683) 62233; fax (017683) 62211; mobile (04216) 46801; e-mail info@toursofdiscovery.demon.co.uk; website http://www.cumbria.com/cumbrian.

Some local companies also provide customized tours in minibuses that seat 8–12 people and will pick you up at your hotel. One of the largest is Mountain Goat Tours, Victoria Street, Windermere LA23 1AD; Tel. (015394) 45161; fax (015394) 45164; e-mail mountaingoat@lakes-pages.co.uk; website http://www.lakes-pages.co.uk. The National Trust offers half-day landscape tours from May through October; these leave from Bridge House at Ambleside and Lakeside at Keswick.

H

HEALTH and MEDICAL CARE

The National Health Service offers free emergency treatment or first aid to all visitors to the United Kingdom. This does not apply to dental treatment or to visits to an optician. For treatment of a more complicated nature or for a pre-existing condition, charges will be made. It is always sensible to take out comprehensive insurance in the event of a serious health problem. Your travel agent will be able to help you find a moderately priced travel insurance policy that includes some degree of medical coverage. Many over-the-counter drugs are available for everyday ailments. Most towns have a chemist or a dispensing chemist shop (pharmacy), with qualified pharmacists on staff who can offer advice about the product you might need.

L

LANGUAGE

Transatlantic and transcontinental differences in word choice are more numerous than you might think, especially for some very common terms. Here is a list of some of the words commonly confused by British and American speakers of English (see also DRIVING):

British	American
bill	check (restaurant)
bonnet	hood (of car)
boot	trunk (of car)
caravan	trailer
chemist	druggist
first floor	second floor
lay-by	roadside parking space
lorry	truck
off-license	liquor store
nappy	diaper
pavement	sidewalk
queue	stand in line
return	round-trip (ticket)
single	one-way (ticket)

lift	elevator
tube or **underground**	subway

M

MAPS

The Ordnance Survey series of maps are the best for visitors interested in walking the fells; they are extremely detailed and offer a variety of scales. For general touring there are a number of easy-to-use maps available at tourist offices and bookshops. The Cumbria Tourist Board produces a comprehensive touring map that also has street maps for the major towns, cultural information, and useful telephone numbers.

MEDIA

The main regional newspaper, the *Westmoreland Gazette,* is the best source for events in the arts, entertainment, sports, and nightlife.

The main national dailies are the *Times,* the *Telegraph,* and the *Guardian,* all of which cover world events. Daily tabloids include the *Sun* and the *Daily Mirror.* A number of newsagents sell foreign newspapers, particularly in the summer months. These include Whittakers and The Post Office in Ambleside and W H Smiths in Windermere.

Although there are five television channels operating in the UK, much of the Lake District receives only four: BBC1, BBC2, ITV, and Channel 4. Very few hotels provide satellite service, though some offer Sky, which has 24-hour news; ask before making a reservation if you need these services. BBC radio stations cover the gamut from pop music and easy listening to current affairs, sports, and classical music.

MONEY MATTERS

Currency. The monetary unit is the pound sterling (£), divided into 100 pence (p). *Banknotes:* £5, £10, £20, £50. *Coins:* 1p, 2p, 5p, 10p, 20p, 50p, £1, and £2.

Currency exchange. All major banks provide currency exchanges, as do the major branches of the Post Office and some travel agencies. The travel agencies normally display a tariff board in the window to show current rates of exchange. Only a few hotels in the Lake District are able to exchange currency for their guests.

Lake District

Credit cards. Credit cards are widely accepted in shops, restaurants, and hotels, but not always in small B&B's and pubs. If you plan to stay in budget accommodations, it's best to check beforehand.

ATMs. Automatic teller machines, dispensing cash to holders of Cirrus cards and major credit cards, are increasing in number. You will find them in Cockermouth, Keswick, Penrith, Ambleside, Bowness, Kendal, and Windermere. Each machine indicates which cards it accepts.

Traveler's checks. Traveler's checks are widely accepted throughout the region.

OPENING HOURS

Standard opening hours are 9am–5pm Monday–Friday. This applies to all government offices, though the tourist information centers are open later throughout the week and on weekends, especially in summer.

Banks. Minimum hours are 9am–3:30pm Monday–Friday, although some are open later on weekdays and Saturday morning as well.

Restaurants. Most are generally open noon–2pm and 6pm–10pm, though these hours are shorter in winter, longer in summer. Some establishments close completely for part of the winter. Pubs that sell food generally serve lunch noon–2pm and dinner 7pm–9pm.

Shops. Most shops are open from 9am–5:30pm Monday–Friday; some are open later, as well as on Sunday, in the summer.

POLICE

British policemen have a reputation around the world for their friendliness and their ability to give people directions. In reality the picture is pretty accurate, although in country areas you will not find a policeman on every street corner. If you need the police, find a telephone box and dial 999. You will be connected to an operator who will put you in touch with the emergency service that you need.

POST OFFICES

The main post offices in the large towns provide mailing services, currency exchange, and cash transfer, and sell items such as phone cards. The Royal Mail Service, which transports and delivers mail, is extremely reliable. Opening hours are 9am–5pm Monday–Friday and 9am–12:30pm on Saturday. In outlying areas you'll find sub-post offices that also function as small stores; these do not usually have currency exchange or cash transfer facilities.

The cost of sending a postcard: within the UK, 26p and Europe; to Ireland, 26p; to Australia, Canada, New Zealand, or South Africa, 43p.

PUBLIC HOLIDAYS

Public holidays are generally known as "Bank Holidays" in the UK.

> 1 January
> Good Friday
> Easter Monday
> First Monday in May
> Last Monday in May
> Last Monday in August
> Christmas Day
> Boxing Day (26 Dec, or the first working day after 25 Dec)

PUBLIC TRANSPORTATION (see also BUDGETING FOR YOUR TRIP)

Public transportation can be an attractive alternative to traveling everywhere by car. The Cumbria County Council offers a very comprehensive service called "Journey Planner," which helps you coordinate the many bus, rail, and boat services in the Lake District. This should be your first port of call for any query about transport; Tel. (01228) 606-000; Monday–Friday 9am–5pm, Saturday 9am–noon. This service is also available on the Internet at http://www.cumbria.gov.uk. Written requests should be sent to Cumbria Journey Planner, Chambers, Carlisle, Cumbria CA3 8SG, UK.

Buses. A range of special ticket deals are available for Stagecoach Cumberland bus services throughout the Lake District; these include one- and four-day Explorer tickets, which allow unlimited travel.

Lake District

The main tourist information centers sell Explorer tickets and details about timetables.

Stagecoach Cumbria also operates many regular routes that run through picturesque parts of the National Park; the Keswick to Buttermere route, for example, goes via Honister Pass, and many open-top buses travel on the Windermere to Grasmere route. For information call Stagecoach Cumberland direct at (01946) 63222 Monday–Saturday 7am–7pm, Sunday 9am–5:30pm.

The National Trust offers "Relax and Ride" landscape tours from May to October from Ambleside or Keswick; for details, Tel. (015394) 35599.

The "Freedom of the Lake" ticket on Lake Windermere combines a trip on a lake cruiser, entrance to the Aquarium of the Lakes, and a ride on the Lakeside and Haverthwaite Railway. Post Bus Services run between Penrith and Patterdale, between Ulverston and Grizedale, and between Broughton-in-Furness and the Duddon Valley; timetables can be obtained from Cumbria Journey Planner.

T

TELEPHONE

When making an international call, dial 00 before the country code.

The country code for the United Kingdom (for calling from other countries) is 44. Here are the international codes when calling from the United Kingdom:

Australia	61
Canada	1
Ireland	353
New Zealand	64
South Africa	27
US	1

Phone calls can be make from call boxes and kiosks using coins, credit cards, and calling cards (some of the older boxes may only accept coins). Phone cards can be purchased from newsagents, post offices, and tourist information offices. To make a telephone call, first insert the coins, phone card, or credit card in the appropriate slot, then follow the instructions on the visual display.

Calls can also usually be made direct from hotel rooms but do ask about the phone charges in advance, as hotel rates are often much higher than normal direct-call tariffs.

TIME ZONES

Eastern Standard Time in the US and Canada is 5 hours behind Greenwich Mean Time; Pacific Coastal Time is 8 hours behind. Sydney, Australia, is 10 hours ahead of Greenwich Mean Time. South Africa is two hours ahead.

TIPPING

Most hotels and restaurants add a service charge of 10%–15% to the bill, and a further tip is not required. If service has not been satisfactory this charge may be deducted. If the establishment does not automatically add a service charge, there should be a note to that effect printed on the bill; a tip of 10%–15% is generally adequate. A tip of £3–£4 per week is adequate for maid service in hotels; hotel porters are typically given 50p per bag. Taxi drivers and hairdressers do not have service charges included in their bills; 10%–15% is acceptable for satisfactory service.

TOILETS

Most towns and villages in the Lake District have free public toilets available to walkers and ramblers. They are generally clean (if a little cold in the winter), but they may have wet and muddy floors when it's raining. You'll typically find signs pointing to the toilets in town centers or near information points.

TOURIST INFORMATION OFFICES

The Cumbria Tourist Board distributes information on the Lake District, as well as on much of the rest of the county of Cumbria. For information on attractions and accommodation contact their main office: Cumbria Tourist Board, Ashleigh, Holly Road, Windermere, Cumbria LA23 2AQ; Tel. (015394) 44444; fax (015394) 44041; e-mail mail@cumbria-tourist-board.co.uk.

The British Tourist Authority can provide you with information before you leave home:

Lake District

Australia	Level 16 Gateway, 1 Macquarie Place, Sydney, New South Wales 2000; Tel. (2) 9377-4400; fax (2) 9377-4499
Canada	Suite 120, 5915 Airport Road, Mississuaga, Ontario L4V 1T1; Tel. (905) 405 1720; fax (905) 405 8490
Ireland	18/20 College Green, Dublin 2; Tel. (1) 670-8100; fax (1) 670- 8244
New Zealand	3rd Floor, Dilworth Building, Auckland 1; Tel. (9) 303-1446; fax (9) 377-6965
US	Suite 4510, 625 North Michigan Avenue, Chicago, Il 60611-1977; Tel. (312) 787 0464; fax (312) 787 9641
	551 Fifth Avenue, Suite 701, New York, NY 10176-0799; Tel. (212) 986-2266; fax (212) 986-1188
	10880 Wilshire Boulevard, Suite 570, Los Angeles, CA 90024; Tel. (310) 470-2782; fax (310) 470-8549

In London, contact the British Travel Centre, 1 Lower Regent Street, Piccadilly Circus, London SW1Y 4NX; Tel. (0171) 808-3800; open Mon–Fri 9am–6:30pm, Sat–Sun 10am–4pm.

Once you're in the Lake District, you can consult any of the following information centers (all are open year-round):

Ambleside: Buildings, Market Cross, Ambleside LA22 9BS; Tel. (015394) 32582; fax (015394) 34901

Cockermouth: The Town Hall, Cockermouth CA13 9NP; Tel. (01900) 822-634; fax (01900) 822-603

Kendal: The Town Hall, Highgate, Kendal LA9 4DL; Tel. (01539) 725-758; fax (01539) 734-457

Keswick: Moot Hall, Market Square, Keswick CA12 5JR; Tel. (017687) 72645; fax (017687) 75043

Penrith: Robinson's School, Middlegate, Penrith CA11 7PT; Tel. (01768) 867-466; fax (01768) 891-754

Windermere: Victoria Street, Windermere LA23 1AD; Tel. (015394) 46499; fax (015394) 47439

The following towns also have tourist offices that are open only April–November: Bowness-on-Windermere, Coniston, Grasmere, Hawkshead, Pooley Bridge, Seatoller, and Ullswater.

The Cumbria Tourist Board website, http://www.cumbria-the-lake-district.co.uk, has general information about the Lake District along with photographs of some of the most famous lakes and peaks.

Lake District National Park visitor centers in Brockhole, Tel. (105394) 46610, and Seatoller and Whinlatter Pass, Tel. (017687) 78469, have information about the work they do and about guided walks and activities organized by park staff. The National Trust has information centers at Bridge House, Ambleside; Lakeside, Keswick; The Square, Hawkshead; Wordsworth House, Cockermouth; and Fell Foot Country Park, Newby Bridge, where you can find out about the work that the National Trust undertakes to conserve British heritage.

WEBSITES

To help plan your trip to the Lake District, check out these sites:

British Tourist Authority	www.visitbritain.com
Cumbria Tourist Board	www.cumbria-the-lake-district.co.uk
Cumbria County Council	www.cumbria.gov.uk
General Information	www.cumbria.com
Telephone Directory	www.infospace.com/uk.thomw
Telephone Directory	www.yellowpages.co.uk

A number of cities, services, and specific attractions also have sites:

Beatrix Potter	www.peterrabbit.co.uk
British Airways	www.british-airways.com
Hadrian's Wall	www.hadrians-wall.org
Keswick	www.keswick.org
National Express Coaches	www.nationalexpress.com
The Ruskin Foundation	www.airtime.co.uk/ruskin/ruskin.html
Virgin Trains	www.virgintrains.co.uk
Windermere Lake Cruises	www.marketsite.co.uk/lakes
The Wordsworth Trust	www.dovecott.demon.co.uk

WEIGHTS and MEASURES

Britain uses the metric system for weights and measures.

Length

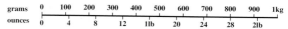

Weight

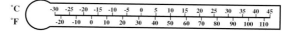

Temperature

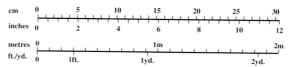

Y

YOUTH HOSTELS

There are over 25 youth hostels in the Lake District. They can be found in the major towns and the more secluded locations, and they range from historic houses to modern buildings to wood cabins. The largest is Ambleside with 226 beds, the smallest Skiddaw with only 15. As is the case with all types of accommodations in the Lake District, they are very popular during the summer months and should always be booked in advance. Details are available from Cumbria Tourist Board (see TOURIST INFORMATION OFFICES). The Youth Hostel Association also offers a mini-bus service between 8 hostels during the summer, for a fee of £2 per journey. This service will also send your rucksack on to your next hostel if you're walking or cycling.

Recommended Hotels

Below is a selection of accommodations in towns and villages throughout the Lake District. It is always advisable to make reservations well in advance, particularly if you will be visiting in high season (late June–mid Sept) or during school holidays (one week in late May and one week in late Oct).

Almost all rooms in the Lake District are priced at a B&B (bed-and-breakfast) rate, per person, with a fee added at many places for individuals traveling alone. Many Lakeland hotels also quote a D, B&B (dinner, bed, and breakfast) rate, which includes the evening meal and is often quite cost-effective.

If you arrive in the Lake District without a reservation, contact one of the information offices of the British Tourist Authority for lists of lodgings and assistance in booking (see ACCOMMODATIONS, page 108, and TOURIST INFORMATION OFFICES, page 125).

If you wish to make a booking before you arrive in the UK, dial 00 44 and then the number of the establishment you require. Remember to use the area code in parentheses beside the telephone number.

The following price guidelines are for bed and breakfast per person per night unless otherwise indicated.

✽✽✽✽✽	Over £100
✽✽✽✽	£60–£100
✽✽✽	£40–£60
✽✽	£25–£40
✽	under £25

THE SOUTHEAST

Ambleside

Ambleside Lodge ✽✽✽-✽✽✽✽ *Rothay Road, Ambleside, LA22 0EJ; Tel. (015394) 31681; fax (015394) 34547; e-mail cherryho@globalnet.co.uk; website www.ambleside-lodge.com.*

Lake District

An elegant house set amid 2½ acres of woodland, within easy walking distance of the town center and the lake. Many different room sizes. Affiliated with a fitness center. 19 rooms. Major credit cards.

Ambleside Salutation Hotel ❋❋❋ *Lake Road, Ambleside, LA22 9BX; Tel. (015394) 32244; fax (015394) 34197.* A relatively large hotel in the heart of Ambleside. Eat in the hotel or explore the restaurants and pubs in town. Well placed for shopping and local transportation. Satellite TV in all rooms. Affiliated with a local fitness center. 36 rooms. Major credit cards.

Grey Friar Lodge ❋❋ *Clappersgate, Ambleside, LA22 9NE; Tel. and fax (015394) 33158; e-mail gflodge@aol.com.* Situated between Ambleside and the Langdales, this pretty little family-run country house offers beautiful views and wonderful hospitality. The restaurant features good home cooking. Cash only.

Kirkstone Foot Hotel ❋❋❋ *Kirkstone Pass Road, Ambleside, LA22 9E; Tel. (015394) 32232; fax (015394) 32805.* A splendid 17th-century manor house in the hills above Ambleside, a five-minute walk from town. The house has been modernized yet retains its original character. The restaurant, renowned for its puddings and sweets, has an extensive menu and wine list. A number of self-catering cottages are also available on the same grounds. 14 rooms. Major credit cards.

Nanny Brow Country House Hotel ❋❋❋❋ *Clappersgate, Ambleside, LA22 9NJ; Tel. (015394) 32036; fax (015394) 32450; e-mail reservations@nannybrowhotel.demon.com.uk.* Situated on the road from Ambleside to the Langdales, this award-winning hotel is just a short walk from the fells and the waterfalls. Wonderful food—English dishes with a Continental twist—and fine wines will restore you after a day spent outdoors. 17 rooms. Major credit cards.

The Regent Hotel ❋❋-❋❋❋ *Waterhead Bay, Ambleside, LA22 0ES; Tel. (015394) 32254; fax (015394) 31474; e-mail* *regent.hotel@cerbernet.co.uk.* An impressive hotel on the banks of Lake Windermere, near the ferry jetty at Waterhead. The heated indoor swimming pool is great for easing aching muscles or keeping the children happy. The restaurant offers dishes made from locally produced ingredients. 30 rooms. Major credit cards.

Bowness

The Blenheim Lodge ❋❋ *Brantfell Road, Bowness-on-Windermere, LA23 3JD; Tel. and fax (015394) 43440; e-mail blenheim@dedicate.co.uk.* A small hotel set above Bowness town with splendid views of the lake, particularly from the rooms at the front of the house. An exclusively non-smoking hotel. The owner is a real character and a gold mine of information. 10 rooms. Major credit cards.

Burn Howe Garden House Hotel ❋❋❋ *Bowness-on-Windermere, LA23 3HH; Tel. (015394) 46226; fax (015394) 47000; e-mail burnhowhotel@btinternet.com.* Just a few minutes on foot from the center of Bowness or Lake Windermere, this charming hotel is well placed for those traveling without a car (though there is ample parking). Guests can choose from three types of rooms: single-story, chalet style, or two-story with balcony. A pleasant restaurant serves English and French cuisine. 26 rooms. Major credit cards.

Lindeth Howe Country House Hotel ❋❋❋ *Lindeth Drive, Longtail Hill, Bowness, LA23 3JF; Tel. (015394) 45759; fax (015394) 46368; e-mail lindeth.howe@kencomp.net; website www.lakes-pages.co.uk.* This house, overlooking Lake Windermere, was once owned by Beatrix Potter—there are pictures in the hotel of her and the staff posing outside the main entrance. A small and relaxed hotel with a dining room overlooking the lake. The rooms in this lodging are of varying size, so ask about the options when you book. Affiliated with a local fitness center. 15 rooms. Major credit cards.

Lake District

Cartmel

The Cavendish Arms at Cartmel ●● *Cartmel, LA11 6QA; Tel. (015395) 36240; fax (015395) 36620; e-mail the cavendish@compuserve.com.* A 15th-century inn with welcoming public bars. The bedrooms are all comfortable but a little small for a long stay; each is quaint in its own way, with features such as sloping floors or stone lintels—as befits the very old building. The food in the pub is extremely good and the portions are huge. 10 rooms. Major credit cards.

Grasmere

The Golden Rill Hotel ●●● *Red Bank Road, Grasmere, LA22 9PU; Tel. (015394) 35486; fax (015394) 35097; e-mail enquiries@gold-ril.com.* Set on grounds adjacent to the lake at Grasmere and only a few minutes walk from the village, the Golden Rill has a heated swimming pool and two acres of lawn and garden to enjoy. The original building of Lakeland stone has been extended and includes a modern bar and restaurant with panoramic views of the garden. 25 rooms. Major credit cards.

Rothay Garden Hotel ●●● *Broadgate, Grasmere, LA22 9RJ; Tel. (015394) 35334; fax (015394) 35723.* On the outskirts of Grasmere village, this elegant house of Cumberland slate has been tastefully extended to include a conservatory restaurant. Bedrooms are cozy and but nicely decorated. Award-winning food. 26 bedrooms. Major credit cards.

Hawkshead

Bowick Lodge ●● *Outgate, Hawkshead, LA22 0PU; Tel. and fax (015394) 36332.* A 17th-century country house set in delightful gardens away from the bustle of the towns, this small award-winning hotel has the feel of a family home. Home-cooked food and a relaxed atmosphere. Non-smoking establishment. 6 rooms. Major credit cards.

Highfield House Country Hotel ●●● *Hawkshead Hill, Near Ambleside, LA22 0PN; Tel. (015394) 36344; fax (015394)*

36793; e-mail *Highfield.Hawkshead@btinternet.com*. A Cumberland-slate country house set among mature gardens. The resident proprietors offer a warm welcome and a menu of traditional English food. 11 rooms. Major credit cards.

The Sawrey House Country Hotel ✿✿✿ *Near Sawrey, Hawkshead, LA22 0LF; Tel. (015394) 36387; fax (015394) 36010; e-mail sawreyhouse@aol.com*. With views over the quiet lake of Esthwaite Water, this hotel offers peace and quiet, but it's also convenient to Hill Top, the attractions of Hawkshead and Coniston, and the forest at Grizedale. 11 rooms. Major credit cards.

Lakeside

Lakeside Hotel ✿✿✿-✿✿✿✿ *Newby Bridge,Windermere, LA12 8AT; Tel. (015395) 31207; fax (015395) 31699; e-mail LSHOTEL@aol.com; website www.lakesidehotel.co.uk*. A historic hotel in an imposing setting on the southern tip of Lake Windermere, next to Lakeside Aquarium and beside the lake ferry jetty. Restaurant and brasserie on site. Free use of nearby leisure facilities. 80 rooms. Major credit cards.

Windermere

Holbeck Ghyll Country House Hotel ✿✿✿✿ *Holbeck Lane, Windermere; Tel. (015394) 32375; fax (015394) 34743; e-mail accommodation@holbeck-ghyll.co.uk*. This tastefully refurbished 19th-century hunting lodge provides luxurious and elegant accommodations. Wonderful views of Lake Windermere. Has its own health spa and a popular gourmet restaurant. Major credit cards.

The Gilpin Lodge ✿✿✿-✿✿✿✿ *Crook Road, Windermere, LA23 3NE; Tel. (015394) 88818; fax (015394) 88058; e-mail hotel@gilpin-lodge.co.uk; website www.gilpin-lodge.co.uk*. Situated opposite Windermere Golf Course, and away from the crowds at Bowness, this genteel yet friendly hotel was originally an Edwardian family house. Individually decorated luxurious rooms are complimented by fine cuisine and an extensive wine list. An extremely stylish and comfortable place to stay. Affiliated with local fitness center. 14 rooms. Major credit cards.

Miller Howe Hotel ✪✪✪✪✪ *Rayrigg Road, Windermere, LA23 1EY; Tel. (015394) 42536; fax (015394) 45664; e-mail lakeview@millerhowe.com.* Set in the splendor of an exquisite Edwardian residence, the Miller Howe is one of the premier places to stay in the Lake District. It offers small numbers of guests the opportunity to share in an intimate English country house experience—with the owner serving as host, guests enjoy an evening together over dinner much as you might at a week-end party. Fine furniture and antiques fill the house. Set gourmet menu. D, B&B plan only. 12 rooms. Major credit cards.

Storrs Hall ✪✪✪✪✪ *Lake Windermere, LA23 3LJ; Tel. (015394) 47111; fax (015394) 47555.* This magnificent Georgian house has been refurbished to the highest standards. Set on the banks of Lake Windermere, it offers magnificent views and beautiful gardens. The house is filled with period reproductions and antiques. A real experience of English luxury. 16 rooms. Major credit cards.

THE SOUTHWEST

The Langdale Hotel and Country Club ✪✪✪✪ *The Langdale Estate, Great Langdale, Near Ambleside, LA22 9JD; toll-free Tel. (0500) 051197; fax (015394) 37694; e-mail www.langdale.co.uk.* A beautiful old estate set in the heart of the countryside and offering luxurious accommodations. The hotel boasts a country club with pool and leisure facilities, hairdressers, beauty salon, and choice of two restaurants. Everything you need is on site. 65 rooms. Major credit cards.

THE NORTHEAST

Penrith

The Westmorland Hotel ✪✪ *Orton, Penrith, CA10 8SJ; Tel. (015396) 24351; fax (015396) 24354.* Lying just outside the National Park but within easy reach of the M6 highway, this hotel is a good choice if you arrive in the Lake District late at night and don't want to wander along the country roads in search of lodging. The staff and the large log fire in the lounge are welcoming. Guest rooms are very comfortable. 53 rooms. Major credit cards.

Ullswater

Glenridding Hotel ✿✿✿ *Glenridding, Ullswater, CA11 0PB; Tel. (017684) 82228; fax (017684) 82555.* With views over Ullswater Lake and the surrounding countryside, this large hotel is the hub of activity in Glenridding, with pubs and restaurants that attract a lot of public trade. Hotel facilities include a swimming pool. 40 rooms. Major credit cards.

The Sharrow Bay Country House Hotel ✿✿✿✿✿ *Lake Ullswater, Penrith, CA10 2LZ; Tel. (017684) 86301; fax (017684) 86349.* The Sharrow Bay was the first country house hotel in the Lake District, and it is still considered by many to be the best. Good hospitality, fantastic views over the lake, and wonderful gourmet food and wine all combine to make this a very special place to stay. D, B&B plan only. 26 rooms. Major credit cards.

THE NORTHWEST

Buttermere

The Bridge Hotel ✿✿✿ *Buttermere, CA13 9UZ; Tel. (017687) 70252; fax (017687) 70215.* Situated between Buttermere and Crummock Water, this hotel, with welcoming log fires in the public rooms, is popular with members of the walking fraternity on summer weekends. Restaurant and pub food. 22 rooms. Major credit cards.

Borrowdale

The Borrowdale Gates Country House Hotel ✿✿✿ *Grange-in-Borrowdale, Keswick, CA12 5UQ; Tel. (017687) 77204; fax (017687) 77254.* A large slate house, nestling at the entrance to the Borrowdale Valley. Rooms have panoramic views of the surrounding countryside. A comfortable hotel with friendly service, this is also a popular place for Sunday lunch and afternoon tea. 28 rooms. Major credit cards.

The Leathes Head Hotel ❋❋❋ *Borrowdale, CA12 5UY; Tel. (017687) 77247; fax (017687) 77363; e-mail www.leatheshead. co.uk.* A refurbished Edwardian country house of Cumberland slate set in private grounds in the valley of Borrowdale. Magnificent views of the surrounding countryside. 11 rooms. Major credit cards.

Cockermouth

Lakeland Sheep and Wool Centre ❋❋ *Egremont Road, Cockermouth, CA13 0QX; Tel. and fax (01900) 822673.* It might seem like an unlikely place to stay, but the modern, motel-style rooms here are a good value—prices are fixed per room rather than per person. All rooms have en-suite facilities and satellite TV. Café and restaurant on site. Just a five-minute drive from Cockermouth. 12 rooms. Major credit cards.

The Trout Hotel ❋❋❋ *Crown Street, Cockermouth, CA13 0EJ; Tel. (01900) 823591; fax (01900) 827514.* On the shores of the River Derwent, this hotel makes a comfortable base for exploring the northwestern lakes. It has an elegant Georgian-style dining room and 15th-century bars and lounges. The modern extension at the rear of the hotel has some very spacious rooms. 29 rooms. Major credit cards.

Keswick

Armathwaite Hall Hotel ❋❋❋❋ *Bassenthwaite Lake, Keswick, CA12 4RE; Tel. (017687) 76551; fax (017687) 76220.* This luxurious, tastefully decorated hotel sits in a fantastic setting of 400 acres on the banks of the lake. An equestrian center and the Trotters and Friends Animal Farm are nearby. There are 16 family rooms and a daily activity program for children. Fine cuisine. Fitness club and beauty salon. 42 rooms. Major credit cards.

Cottage in the Wood Hotel ✹✹ *Whinlatter Pass, Braithwaite, Keswick, CA12 5TW; Tel. (017687) 78409.* A 17th-century former coach house in Whinlatter Forest Park. This cozy, family-run hotel is within steps of fine walking and hiking trails and provides easy access to the attractions of the northern lakes. 7 rooms. Major credit cards.

Derwentwater Hotel ✹✹✹✹ *Portinscale, Keswick, CA12 5RE; Tel. (017687) 72538; fax (017687) 71002; e-mail derwent-water.hotel@dial.pipex.com.* The magnificent setting of this hotel, on the lake-shore of Derwentwater, secures it as one of the premier places to stay in the Lake District. In addition to individual guest rooms, the hotel also offers a number of self-catering cottages. Panoramic views. 44 rooms. Major credit cards.

Lyzzick Hall Hotel ✹✹✹ *Underskiddaw, Keswick, CA12 4PY; Tel. (017687) 72277; fax (017687) 72278.* A relaxed, family-run hotel between Keswick town and the base of Skiddaw peak. Pretty gardens surrounded by coniferous forest; good views across the Derwent valley. Indoor heated swimming pool. 29 rooms. Major credit cards.

Swinside Lodge Hotel ✹✹✹ *Newlands, Keswick, CA12 5UE; Tel. and fax (017687) 72948.* A beautiful country house nestling in extensive grounds, within easy reach of Derwentwater Lake, the Swinside Lodge is furnished to a high standard. 7 rooms. Major credit cards.

Thirlmere

Dale Head Hall Lakeside Hotel ✹✹✹ *Lake Thirlmere, Keswick, CA12 5RQ; Tel. (017687) 72478; fax (017687) 71070; e-mail holidayadale-head-hall.co.uk,* A refurbished 16th-century manor house on the shores of Lake Thirlmere, this hotel is in a secluded setting, yet lies within easy reach of the main arterial route through the lakes. It offers a tranquil and relaxed atmosphere for a small number of guests. Small restaurant offering local dishes. 9 rooms. Major credit cards.

Recommended Restaurants

Restaurants in Britian aren't usually open for breakfast, since most visitors eat the meal in their hotel. In summer it's best to call ahead to make reservations; in the off-season you'll probably only need do so on the weekends. Most restaurants offer a set-price *table d'hôte* menu at lunch and dinner as well as an á la carte evening menu.

Many pubs offer a selection of dishes and daily specials. For those on a budget, pubs are often the best choice for good inexpensive fare. Having your main meal at lunchtime is a good way stay on budget; lunches are almost always cheaper than evening meals, and the food is just as good.

Many formal restaurants have age limits for children, or may serve early meals for young guests. Check when you call to make a reservation.

Prices quoted are per person for a three-course meal without drinks. Some of these restaurants offer a *table d'hote* menu of more than three courses.

✪✪✪✪	£40–£50
✪✪✪	£25–40
✪✪	£15–£25
✪	under £15

THE SOUTHEAST

Ambleside

Bertrams Restaurant ✪✪ *Market Place, Ambleside; Tel. (015394) 32119.* Open daily 6–10pm, May–Oct until 10:30pm; closed last three weeks in Jan. This delightful bistro-style restaurant housed in the old meat market in the heart of Ambleside serves a variety of steaks, pasta, and pizza in a casual atmosphere. Good range of beers from around the world. Major credit cards.

The Glass House ✺✺✺ *Rydal Road, Ambleside, LA22 9AN; Tel. (015394) 32137.* Open daily. The modern dining room in this converted water-mill behind Bridge House has something for everyone—traditional English standbys alongside southeast Asian, New World, and vegetarian dishes. Simple lunches are served all day until 5pm; the dinner menu, offered from 6:30pm on, is more extensive. Also vegetarian dishes. Major credit cards.

Nanny Brow Country House ✺✺✺ *Clappergate, Ambleside, LA22 9NF; Tel. (015394) 32036; fax (015394) 32450; e-mail reservations@nannybrowhotel.demon.com.uk.* Open daily for dinner only 7:30–8:45pm. This small hotel serves classic French cooking. An elegant dining room and attentive service make for a refined experience. Major credit cards.

White Moss House ✺✺✺ *Rydal Water, Ambleside; Tel. (015394) 35295; fax (015394) 35516.* Open daily at 8pm for dinner only. This small restaurant with a country cottage ambiance sits on the main road that runs past Rydal Water, just a few minutes drive from Ambleside town. Seasonal menu of English dishes made when possible with local produce. Major credit cards.

Bowness

The Porthole ✺✺✺ *3 Ash Street, Bowness, LA23 3EB; Tel. (015394) 42793.* Open for lunch daily except Tue and Sat, for dinner daily except Tue; close mid Dec–mid Feb. Housed in a converted 17th-century cottage on one of the most charming streets in Bowness, this restaurant with rough stone walls offers a mixture of English, Italian, and French dishes in cozy surroundings. Vegetarian selections are also available. Italian offerings dominate the wine list. Major credit cards.

Cartmel

The Cavendish ✺✺ *Cartmel, LA11 6QA; Tel. (015395) 36240.* Open daily noon–2pm and 6:30–9pm. This 15th-century inn in the center of Cartmel village has cozy log fires in its two main rooms. Lunch and dinner can be also taken in the bar. The menu concentrates on English and Continental selections as well as roast meats, all served in large portions; lighter snacks and pub meals are also available. A good choice of real ales at the bar.

Uplands Hotel ❁❁❁ *Haggs Lane, Cartmel, LA11 6HD; Tel. (015395) 36248; fax (015395) 36848.* Lunch at 1pm Thu–Sun, dinner at 8pm except Mon; closed Jan–Mar. One of the most popular restaurants in the area, the Uplands has one seating for lunch and one for dinner. Large portions of fine English food—roast meats, fresh fish, and seasonal vegetables. Major credit cards.

Grasmere

Michael's Nook ❁❁❁❁ *Grasmere, LA22 9RP; Tel. (015394) 35496.* Open daily, with one seating at 12:30pm for lunch and one at 7:30pm for dinner. Turn right off the main road (A591) at the Swan Hotel and bear left for 400 yards. Part of a country house hotel, this restaurant has excellent dishes that make use of carefully chosen, high-quality ingredients—foie gras and truffles are used regularly. Extensive wine list. Major credit cards.

The Swan ❁❁ *Grasmere, LA22 9RF; Tel. (015394) 35551; fax (015394) 35741.* Open daily noon–2pm and 7–9:30pm. Right on route A591 (the main highway through the Lakes), this 300-year-old coach house, one of Wordsworth's haunts, offers a fine menu of English specialties.

Hawkshead

The Queens Head Hotel ❁❁❁ *Main Street, Hawkshead Village, LA22 0NS; Tel. (015394) 36271.* Open daily noon–2pm and 7–9pm. At this 16th-century inn, complete with original beams and warm log fires, choose between a dinner in the full-service restaurant or lighter fare in the bar. The food is highly acclaimed. Major credit cards.

Kendal

Moon ❁❁ *129 High Gate, Kendal, LA9 4EN; Tel. (01539) 729254.* Open daily for dinner only; closed Christmas, New Year's Day, last week in Jan through first two weeks in Feb. This bistro-style restaurant on Kendal's main thoroughfare serves an eclectic menu of meat, fish, and vegetarian dishes that defy strict categorization. An interesting selection of beers and a wine list with some good values. Major credit cards.

Troutbeck

The Queens Head ❀❀ *Town Head, Troutbeck, LA23 1PW; Tel. (015394) 32174.* Open daily noon–2pm and 6:30–9pm. A traditional "olde-worlde" inn with flagstone floors and log fires, the Queens Head serves carefully prepared, straightforward English standbys. The puddings, served in large portions, are renowned. The bar serves some fine ales and microbrews. Major credit cards.

Windermere

The Gilpin Lodge ❀❀❀-❀❀❀❀ *Crook Road, Windermere, LA23 3NE; Tel. (015394) 88818.* Open daily noon–2:30pm and 7–8:45pm. This fine country hotel has three intimate dining areas; lunch and afternoon tea can be taken in one of the elegant lounges. Superb food with a range of influences, beautifully presented and accompanied by a carefully selected wine list. Major credit cards.

Holbeck Ghyll ❀❀❀ *Holbeck Lane, Windermere, LA23 1LU; Tel. (015394) 32375.* Open daily noon–2pm and 7–9pm. Guests at this renowned country-house hotel and restaurant enjoy local game and meats featured on a menu of English and Continental dishes. A combination of setting and fine food that's hard to beat. Major credit cards.

Jerichos ❀❀❀ *Birch Street, Windermere, LA23 1EG; Tel. (015394) 42522.* Open Tue–Sun for dinner only. This modern bistro-style restaurant with its dramatic decor, brightly painted walls, hip ambiance, and open-plan kitchen stands out from the more traditional Lake District restaurants. The simple menu includes English, Spanish, and Italian dishes. Major credit cards.

The Masons Arms ❀ *Strawberry Bank, Cartmel Fell, Windermere; Tel. (015395) 68486.* Open daily noon–2pm and 7–9pm. Situated at the confluence of several small roads to the

141

east of Lake Windermere, this old-fashioned spot serves plain but delicious English pub food, and lots of it. They also stock over 200 beers from around the world. Stone floors, log fires, and lots of atmosphere.

The Miller Howe Hotel ✿✿✿✿ *Rayrigg Road, Windermere, LA23 1EY; Tel. (015394) 42536.* Open daily, with one seating at 1pm for lunch and one at 8pm for dinner; closed Jan. Top-notch food and wine and breathtaking views over Lake Windermere from all the public rooms. English dishes with Continental influences. Major credit cards.

Roger's Restaurant ✿✿ *4 High Street, Windermere, LA32 1AF; Tel. (015394) 44954.* Open Mon–Sat for dinner only, 7–9:30pm. A well-established restaurant in the center of Windemere, close to the railway station. Roger himself works hard in the kitchen to produce intriguing English and French dishes, including several vegetarian options. In addition to the good-value fixed-price dinner, there are several á la carte options. Major credit cards.

THE SOUTHWEST

Coniston Water

Jumping Jenny Tea Rooms and Brasserie ✿ *Brantwood, Coniston Water; Tel. (015394) 41715.* Open Apr–mid Nov daily 10:30–6pm, mid Nov–Mar Wed–Sun 11am–4pm. This small brasserie is housed in what was once an old stable block at Brantwood. Warming log fires inside will cheer you up in winter, and in summer you can enjoy your food on a sun terrace in front of the building. This is a good place to stop for lunch after a lake cruise and before touring the house. The menu ranges from sandwiches and snacks to pies and stews and includes some vegetarian dishes.

Wast Water

Wasdale Head Inn ✿✿✿ *Wasdale Head, Gosforth; Tel. (019467) 26229.* Open daily noon–2pm and 7–9pm; closed mid

Nov–mid Mar. A welcome sight for many fell walkers as they descend from the higher slopes, this place is often full of hardy types decked out in Gore-Tex. Equally welcoming to those who make the journey by car from Windermere or Ambleside, the inn offers a limited menu of imaginative dishes that make ample use of local ingredients. Good wines and real ale.

THE NORTHEAST

Penrith

Passepartout ✷✷✷ *51 Castlegate, Penrith; Tel. (01768) 65852.* Open Mon–Sat for dinner only. The owner of this small restaurant in an 18th-century building specializes in fish but offers a selection of meat dishes as well; there are also vegetarian dishes on the menu. In summer you can eat on the terrace behind the restaurant. Major credit cards.

Ullswater

The Sharrow Bay Hotel ✷✷✷✷ *Sharrow Bay, Ullswater, CA10 2LZ; Tel. (017684) 86301.* Open daily for lunch at 1pm and dinner at 8pm; closed Dec–late Feb. The Sharrow Bay Country House Hotel was the first of its type in the Lake District, and it still maintains its excellent standards. The cooking here is done in the grand style—hearty traditional Lakeland ingredients like pheasant, venison, and lamb served in large portions. Afternoon tea is splendid here, complimented by some of the prettiest views in the area. Major credit cards.

THE NORTHWEST

Borrowdale

Borrowdale Gates Hotel ✷✷✷ *Grange-in-Borrowdale, Keswick, CA12 5UQ; Tel. (017687) 77204; fax (017687) 77254.* Open daily 12:15–1:30pm and 7–8:45pm. This hotel with views of Borrowdale changes its menu daily, using many local ingredients. Game is a speciality, and there's a good selection of local cheeses. Professional, friendly service. Major credit cards.

Lake District

The Yew Tree ✿✿-✿✿✿ *Seatoller, Borrowdale; Tel. (017687) 77634.* Open Tue–Sun noon–2pm and 7–9pm; closed Fri lunch and through Jan. Dating from the early 1600's, this inn emphasizes local produce, simply cooked and delicious. Lamb, salmon, and duck are favorites. The slate floors, low-beamed ceilings, and open fire create a warm and intimate ambiance, and the service is cheerful and efficient. Major credit cards.

Buttermere

The Bridge Hotel ✿✿-✿✿✿ *Buttermere, CA13 9UZ; Tel. (017687) 70252.* Open daily; dinner in restaurant at 8:30pm. The Bridge offers both a full restaurant menu and bar food. You can't go wrong either way: excellent dishes of locally produced meat and traditional Cumbrian specialties are complemented by vegetarian options. A very popular place in the summer when walkers and those out for a drive converge here for lunch. Major credit cards.

Cockermouth

Quince and Medlar ✿✿ *13 Castlegate, Cockermouth, CA13 9EU; Tel. (01900) 823579.* Open Tue–Sun for dinner only 7–9pm; closed Nov and late Jan–early Feb; closed Sun from New Year's Eve to Easter. An award-winning vegetarian restaurant on a corner near the castle and brewery. Most of the customers are not vegetarians, which says something about the quality of the food.

Keswick

Underscar Manor ✿✿✿✿ *Applethwaite, Keswick,CA12 4PH; Tel. (017687) 75000; fax (017687) 74904.* Open daily noon–1pm and 7–8:30pm.With seating for 50, this restaurant, set in an impressive Italianate house, is relatively large by Lake District standards. The lavish decorations of the dining room put guests in the mood to enjoy the manor's dependable performance of exciting food and professional service. Major credit cards.